L. SHANNON JUNG

Building the
GOOD LIFE
for All

Transforming Income Inequality
in Our Communities

WJK WESTMINSTER
JOHN KNOX PRESS
LOUISVILLE · KENTUCKY

For ALICE

First edition
Published by Westminster John Knox Press
Louisville, Kentucky

17 18 19 20 21 22 23 24 25 26—10 9 8 7 6 5 4 3 2 1

Book design by Drew Stevens
Cover design by Barbara LeVan Fisher, www.levanfisherdesign.com

Library of Congress Cataloging-in-Publication Data
Names: Jung, L. Shannon (Loyle Shannon), 1943– author.
Title: Building the good life for all : transforming income inequality in our communities /
   L. Shannon Jung.
Description: Louisville, KY : Westminster John Knox Press, 2017.
Identifiers: LCCN 2017006619 (print) | LCCN 2017029756 (ebook) |
   ISBN 9781611648195 (ebk.) | ISBN 9780664263188 (pbk. : alk. paper)
Subjects: LCSH: Church work with the poor—United States. | Poor—Religious
   aspects—Christianity. | Community development—Religious aspects—Christianity. |
   Income distribution.
Classification: LCC BV639.P6 (ebook) | LCC BV639.P6 J86 2017 (print) |
   DDC 261.8/325—dc23
LC record available at https://lccn.loc.gov/2017006619

Most Westminster John Knox Press books are available at special quantity discounts when purchased in bulk by corporations, organizations, and special-interest groups. For more information, please e-mail SpecialSales@wjkbooks.com.

CONTENTS

ACKNOWLEDGMENTS

The book is indebted to many. For sabbatical support, for the students in its Leading the Affluent Church course, for professional collegiality, and for so much more, I am very grateful to Saint Paul School of Theology, Kansas City. La Salle University and Saint Vincent School of Theology in Manila were our host institutions when Patti and I taught in the Philippines for a semester. This book benefited from our living in a slum where we had to step over people sleeping on the sidewalk when we went to the market. Thanks to Drs. Agnes Brazal and Jeane Perracullo, who made our stay fruitful and stimulating. The topic of this book was also very much at the forefront of my mind when I received a Bridwell Fellowship to wallow around the fine facility at the Bridwell Library, Perkins School of Theology.

Here in Florida, the members of the classes I taught at First Presbyterian Church, Sarasota, and also my home church, Peace Presbyterian, Lakewood Ranch, were guinea pigs for the chapters of this book and were particularly helpful in pointing me to organizations that were aiming to empower ALICE.

A group that calls itself the ALICE project is working on a video and a Web site with the domain name www.working hardtogetby.org that is rough but also ready to be enjoyed. That group includes especially Grant Lowe and Karen Windom but also officials with the United Way here in Bradenton—Philip Brown, Bronwyn Beightol, and Bruce Meyer, as well as Debby

Sunkenberg and Ryan Bremner. I have also learned much from working at Turning Points, a one-stop service center for the homeless, in Bradenton.

Dr. Nancy Barry, a member of the English department at Luther College in Iowa and a creative writer, helped edit every word of this book and vastly improved its flow and readability. She is a marvel. Thanks are also due Karen O'Dowd, Dotty and David Thomas, and others who read and critiqued. Jessica Miller Kelley at Westminster John Knox Press not only contributed valuable suggestions that improved the book but also guided the book toward a tighter focus. Thanks as well to Julie Tonini and the rest of the production team at WJK who added their expertise.

Finally, of course, but also first, is my wife and colleague and co-dishwasher, Dr. Patricia Beattie Jung, who makes life adventurous and fun. God be thanked.

INTRODUCTION

As a teacher and pastor, I have been drawn to those who lacked daily necessities. I have examined and taught about poverty, have thought about how pastors might address financial issues in their communities, have even written about how to deal with hunger issues. Maybe that came from being the child of educational and dental missionaries in the Congo. I have been involved in housing ministries, food banks, and community organizing. As that work has gone on, I have come to realize that it is not just those officially below the poverty line who are struggling.

When I retired and moved to Florida, I thought that this was the land of prosperity and opportunity, or at least of economic stability. I expected, since every time we vacationed there was a jovial and carefree spirit, that everyone was financially stable here in the land of sunshine and tourism. Living here punctured that illusion. How wrong I was. Indeed, peeling back the cover of worker friendliness, we discovered the same issues that we had known in Kansas City, Chicago, and Dubuque. There are a lot of people working hard and just

barely getting by. These are blue-collar, hardworking people who can just barely pay their bills. Many of them are African American or Hispanic, but the majority are white men and women. They are single women living in their cars to save money to go back to school, hoping for a better life for themselves; couples working two or three jobs to make ends meet and trying to raise their children as well. The income gap is only superficially invisible.

As Americans we are dealing with a new economic reality. It is not just the homeless and unemployed who live hand to mouth. The working poor are living paycheck to paycheck. Their futures are anything but secure. The reality of the number of employed, hardworking people who nonetheless struggle financially degrades our collective sense of well-being. Our well-being is eroded by the sheer magnitude of this problem and the plight of lower-income working people. This group is twice as large as the officially defined poor. Increasingly the middle class is becoming the working poor, and the economic plight of millions of Americans has become a major national concern.

Shortly after we arrived in Florida there was a report of a study done by the United Way in Manatee and Sarasota Counties. It investigated the percentage of people who are Asset-Limited, Income-Constrained, Employed (ALICE); that is, the working poor. To avoid the impression that all the working poor are female, I am also using the acronym ALEC (Asset-Limited, Employed, Constrained) interchangeably with ALICE. The vulnerability of this group of people does not know any one gender. In Manatee and Sarasota Counties respectively, 30 and 29 percent of the population have income above the poverty level but not enough to meet the cost of living. Added to those who live in poverty, 43 and 41 percent of the people in these two counties are struggling to get by. They are fairly representative of the findings of the six-state United Way report. My illusions seemed pretty naive in the wake of that report.

The United Way report points toward a new definition of poverty. The reality is that close to 50 percent of the people in the United States are struggling hard to get by. The working

poor may now be the new majority. The income instability of many citizens was also revealed in the election campaign of 2016. The stagnation of the economy ripped through political customs that have papered over the fact that many are just not making it in America anymore. For too long many have thought that suppressing their fear would keep a personal financial crisis at bay. The symptoms are apparent: middle-aged white people dying from depression, drug overdoses, alcoholism, and other anxiety-related illnesses in greater numbers; the addition of new jobs but ones that do not pay decently; the vast difference in *wealth* among African Americans, Hispanics, Asians, and whites.

Senator Bernie Sanders, campaigning to be the Democratic nominee for president, blew the cover off the plight of men and women who are working hard and living on the edge. Donald Trump used the rage of the working white man and woman to swell his candidacy and win the presidency. These are the symptoms of a vast sense that something is wrong in our society. While these are the topics of media attention and are aspects of reality that cannot be ignored, fear is a poor motive. Rage is a dysfunctional response. People wind up feeling frustrated, overwhelmed, immobilized, and encouraged only to look after their own self-interest. Some families are simply seeking a financial foxhole to protect themselves against inevitable forces. This reaction only deepens their fear and dread. It only reinforces the sense that we cannot do anything about this.

Rather than move into fear, our response as Christians to what is happening is to become proactive. We are called to consider the Christian ideal of interdependence and do some real work to reverse the disparity. While it would be unrealistic to ignore the reality of the new poverty, our intention is to point to those individuals and activities that are making positive change. There are numerous points of light, if you will, that are joyfully pushing back against the sense of inevitability. David King, the director of the Lake Institute on Faith and Giving, writes that "religious institutions need not live out of a scarcity mind-set. Our religious communities are full of the necessary assets to cultivate a culture of generosity."[1]

I have three goals in this book.

First, show that we are all interdependent. We are all in this together. We all breathe the same air. We all depend on clean water, as the residents of Flint, Michigan, can tell you only too well. We are all, in fact, threatened by the sort of contamination and illness that happened there. We seem to be facing more floods, increasingly strong storms, and more weather events like tornadoes in this decade. We are all impacted by the global economy and climate change. The destinies of the wealthy and of the poor are converging in other ways, such as the safety of the global food system, and will ultimately impact us all. Similarly, the programs and organizations we highlight in this book are universal—they are geared ultimately to benefit all of us. For example, public education has a direct impact on all of us.

Second, demonstrate that the growing income gap impacts our spirituality as well. Beyond our environmental and social interdependence is the interrelated state of our spirituality. This is the case for both rich and poor, employed and unemployed. How we respond to our situations is integrally tied into our spirituality, which includes both how we respond to others and also our own character. Even those who are not self-aware exhibit a spirituality that is either life enriching or life diminishing. We are alert to the situation of others or we turn a blind eye to it. That impacts our spiritual well-being.

What we seek to do here is to encourage ourselves and you toward a spirituality that enables us to flourish. Many religions embrace such a spirituality. We are persuaded that this is a Christian vision, though we would not at all deny that other religions point in the same direction. It is quite clear that Christianity and many other religions include at their core a compassion toward others and also commend a society where all people have enough to enjoy a decent life. The God we worship is a God of abundance who freely gives to all.

Third, introduce four strategies for addressing income instability in your own context. We have models for this work; chapters 3–6 describe organizations, programs, and actions that are already contributing to human flourishing. The chapters outline four strategies:

— *Relief*, also called charity, gives goods or services to those in desperate straits to meet immediate needs.
— *Self-help* empowers people in their own development through education, mentoring, and a stable foundation from which to succeed.
— *Cultural formation* creates an ethos for action, focused on large-scale public issues. This involves influencing public opinion, participating in social movements, and encouraging pro-social business policy.
— *Governmental action* uses state and federal policies to promote the well-being and success of those struggling to get by.

A chapter devoted to each describes how organizations that adopt one or more of the strategies help ALICE work toward a decent livelihood. These are programs that you too can get involved with, and I hope to inspire and equip you to take action in your community to address the crisis of income inequality. We who undertook to examine ALICE in our own area of central Florida were upset by the injustices and also the just plain hardships that the working poor experience. In addition to this book, we are launching an online effort to publicize those organizations that are responding to income inequality and helping people to achieve a decent standard of living. (See www.workinghardtogetby.com.) We hope to encourage you to find similar organizations in your community that you can partner with as individuals or as a group. We know the joy of participating in such hands-on efforts, and we are motivated not so much by altruism as by the attraction of seeing people empowered to live stable lives. Study after study indicates that those ordinary citizens who volunteer and assist others to achieve a decent livelihood say that their lives are significantly happier than those not so involved.

This book is designed for groups to study together, learning more about the experience of the working poor and exploring how we as congregations and individuals can promote both material and spiritual flourishing for all people. Each chapter closes with seven to ten questions designed to help you process what you've read and strategize together how you can participate in promoting economic equality. Chapters 3–6, focusing on each of the four strategies, also include lists of suggested resources that can help you find organizations with whom you might partner. Do some homework as you go, so that when you reach chapter 7, you will have more research in hand with which to chart your way forward in ministry to those who struggle economically.

God has called us to love our neighbors as ourselves. We begin by getting to know who those neighbors might be.

CHAPTER 1

INTERDEPENDENCE
AND THE WORKING POOR

ALICE Is Our Neighbor

Who is ALICE? Who is ALEC?

She is the young woman who washes your dishes at that fancy restaurant.

He is my grandfather who didn't plan for retirement and is working as a greeter at Walmart.

He is David, the formerly well-off middle-aged manager who is deemed expendable.

She is Susan, the McDonald's service worker who takes your order.

She is Sheronda, the woman down the street who has just lost her job.

They are our children, who are living hand to mouth after having made some bad choices.

He is Jamal, the worker who makes only $8.25 an hour.

They are our neighbors.

She and he may be you and me one day, if we are not there already.

There are reports that suggest that almost half of us will be working but living in a financially shaky situation for some period of our lives.[1]

The United Way commissioned a six-state study in 2014 to determine how many households in those states, including Florida, were living in the gap between the poverty line and what the United Way terms the "survival line," earning more than the official U.S. poverty rate but less than the basic cost of living in those six states. They discovered that 44 percent of the households in Florida's Central West Coast experienced financial hardship, while only 15 percent were technically under the poverty line. The cost of living in this seven-county area—labeled a "survival budget" or "basic cost of living"—ranged from $49,777 to $53,300 for a family of four. The average gap for ALICE and ALEC ranged from $4,000 to $8,000 below that threshold.

If you were to go about your daily errands in Bradenton, Florida, where I live, or in the town or city where you live, you might not suspect that one of every two people you encounter does not make enough money to meet the basic cost of living there. Fifty percent are not earning what they need to live. For those dining in Panera, the percentage is probably less. For those shopping in Walmart, the percentage is probably more.

How about your community? How many people there live on less than a survival budget? The issue is not just that a large number of people are the working poor but that we as a society are dependent on their labor. So the working poor (ALICE and ALEC) are those who wait on us in restaurants, who are our secretaries and public school teachers, who cook our food, who serve us in stores, who fix our cars, who grow our food, who clean our offices and homes, who landscape our public spaces, and who work on our highways. We are economically interdependent with them, and the well-being of all of us is tied up in everyone's being able to live decently. We are interdependent, and increasingly many of us are living payday to payday.

What Does Economic Instability Feel Like?

Though we are born with different abilities and into divergent circumstances, we are essentially interdependent. Our economic interconnectedness turns malicious when our natural solidarity is so shattered by disparate conditions that some are deprived of what they need to survive and flourish. Let me tell you a story:

Joe got a job with a small firm that laid tile for floors and bathrooms. He learned how to do it well. When work was slack, his boss would have to give him time off. Because his income was not steady, he decided to start his own company. He had his own tools and borrowed money to buy a used truck and other equipment. His workmanship was high quality, contractors gave him more jobs, and he was busy.

Joe, his wife, and their children lived in a home they rented from a citrus grower. His landlord offered him a job on weekends in exchange for free rent. Joe took him up on it and was starting to pay down his loans with the money he saved on rent.

After six months his landlord demanded about $10,000 in back rent.

"Whoa! What are talking about? We agreed I would work for you weekends in exchange for free rent!"

"No. You must have misunderstood me. I never said that."

Joe, very angry, with expletives said: "You sure did! And I don't have $10,000!"

The landlord said, "If I had intended that, I'd have given you a written agreement. The only written agreement is the one where you will pay me $1,480 per month rent. Since you have not paid, you will have to move."

The next day Joe was driving to a job and had an accident that totaled his truck. His insurance did not include replacement coverage. He could not work without the truck. His few savings were gone quickly. Without a job, Joe, his wife, and their children were homeless.

It can happen that fast. One calamity can destabilize a household that is living paycheck to paycheck. It can reverse even a hopeful story. The series of events in Joe's family situation indicate the tightness of our interconnection. What might have been merely an inconvenience to the financially stable became a matter of being able to make a living for Joe. The health and education of his whole family depended on Joe's truck and the trustworthiness of their landlord. The thinness of the margin on which Joe's family was living reveals the fragility and importance of the interconnections.

Other calamities can revolve around the impact of an accident that causes an injury; of being out of work; of having a spouse close out a joint banking account and abandon the family; of sudden medical crises; of being physically exhausted as a result of working multiple jobs, which results in being prone to accidents at work or to explosive outbursts against supervisors. The scenario of being one paycheck away from poverty is one that both the poor and increasingly the middle class know first- or at least secondhand.

Those poised to address this precariousness from a policy perspective tend to be removed from such risk themselves. Former Florida governor and presidential candidate Jeb Bush relayed the facts of the matter to an audience in Detroit on February 3, 2015, saying that "two out of three American households live paycheck to paycheck. Any unexpected expense can push them into financial ruin. We have a record number of Americans on food stamps and living in poverty."[2] Ironically, it was Trump, the wealthiest candidate of all, who went beyond facts to strike an emotional chord with the white working poor, for whom these statistics are a distressing reality.

ALEC Is Us

There is a new poverty that surpasses what we have known to this point. The sheer quantity of widespread economic insecurity and soaring levels of income inequality are unlike anything since the Great Depression. This exacerbates our fear of what may happen to us in the future. "How much risk do I face?"

we may ask ourselves. Mark Rank and Thomas Hirschl have answered that question. In an article titled "Calculate Your Economic Risk," they report that nearly 60 percent of Americans between the ages of twenty and seventy-five will spend at least one year below the official poverty line, and a full 75 percent of us will experience a year below 150 percent of the poverty line.[3] By the current definition, this means that three-quarters of us will experience a year living on $24,030 for a couple.

What that means in terms of living conditions is hard to imagine. It may involve learning what real hunger is, working fourteen-hour days, choosing between dental work and eating out, paying usurious interest rates at a payday loan store to keep the power from being shut off, sending children to school without adequate food or attention—this is the stuff of inequality. It also means working for inadequate wages and perceiving that others are living the high life off your back, buying goods that are so cheap only because you are paid so little. This interdependence can be galling.

If you think this insecurity is far from you (and me), consider this story:

Kathy and her teenage son recently found themselves in an unfamiliar part of town—at the Chattanooga Community Kitchen. Used to living in an upscale part of the city, Kathy came home one night to discover the locks changed on her doors and her husband nowhere to be located. She and her son had been living in her Cadillac Escalade for a week. A resident of one of the city's wealthiest zip codes for years, she came home one day to find that her estranged husband had changed the locks on the couple's McMansion. She hadn't yet consulted an attorney concerning her rights. Kelly and her son had been sleeping in her Cadillac Escalade for more than a week.

The moral of the story? "The homeless aren't always who you think they are," said Mark Williams, the Community Kitchen's case management director. "Just because you're driving an Escalade doesn't mean you have a garage to park it in."[4]

I am sure that this woman figured that her comfortable socioeconomic situation was beyond instability. She probably felt that her wealth put her beyond the reach of poverty, that she was free of such hurdles. This situation revealed, instead, that she was dependent on several relationships and circumstances. The passage between the "have-mores" and those whose incomes fall below the survival level is not hermetically sealed. The affluent cannot insulate themselves from the effects of this disparity. According to Nobel laureate Joseph Stiglitz, inequality impacts us all.

Stiglitz, in his book *The Price of Inequality*, argues that the large gap between the poor and the affluent is preventing an economic recovery from the Great Recession that began in 2007 and has continued for all but the wealthiest.[5] Much has been said about the disappearance of the middle class, as families' incomes drop and they fall into poverty. They primarily live in income segregation (if not racial segregation as well), and unless one consciously focuses on those who wait on tables, staff fast-food restaurants, clean motels, and stock shelves, they can be overlooked; in fact, they become virtually invisible. The long-term concern is that children will fall into the same insecure situation as their parents.

Nearly 15 million children in this country are poor, and 6.5 million of them are extremely poor, living below half the poverty line.[6] The Children's Defense Fund (CDF) estimates the long-term costs to society at $500 billion in lost productivity, government assistance, health care, and incarceration. This daunting figure is, the CDF says, "six times more than the $77 billion investment we propose to reduce child poverty by 60 percent."[7]

What Do We Value?

The choice we are making as a society, theoretically, to pay $500 billion to treat the effects of poverty rather than investing $77 billion to reduce the causes of poverty, reflects a web of moral, social, and political values. There is a divisive sense of antagonism along class lines. The so-called class war has emerged not as a result of intentional division but as a result of ALEC's frustration in the face of this inequality and the simmering sense of fear and threat among the affluent. One sees this quagmire in the anger and sense of being marginalized that fueled the presidential campaign of Donald Trump, and the disconnect between the billionaire populist's voters and his party's establishment. Many pundits were saying that the working poor do not even vote anymore because it seems a waste of time as ALICEs lose their sense of being represented in this democracy, but working-class white men and women turned out to vote for Trump; he identified the rage that has been burning among white working people, and they felt as though someone had at last heard them.

Others who live fairly comfortable lives lament government social services and emphasize a "pull yourself up by the bootstraps" version of the American dream. Yet others throw up their hands and wonder what can be done about the unstable situation many Americans live in.

I am concerned that the culture of consumption will outstrip the culture of civic engagement and our government will adopt policies that further disadvantage the less well-off. Christians should be outraged at the direction our economic distribution has taken. This new type of poverty is widespread. But we can do something about this. Rather than letting the downward spiral continue, many groups — Christians and civil and college and other — *are* doing something about it. They are recalibrating the situation. We can do that as well.

There is clear evidence that this new poverty, however it may be labeled, violates traditional American values such as these:

— fairness
— care for all children
— equal opportunity, mobility, nondiscrimination
— work and making a contribution
— national destiny
— the value and dignity of each life

Not that those values have evaporated; they are being tattered, however.

We as a society are denying poor people, the working poor, and a large number of the middle class a chance to enjoy their lives free from gnawing insecurity. We are jeopardizing our sense of spirituality and responsibility by not treating these people as our neighbors; we do not love them as we love ourselves. Such neglect boomerangs back on the affluent's morality and spirituality.

In his statement on the environment, *Laudato Si'* ("On Care for Our Common Home"), Pope Francis reasserts the interconnection between the health of the environment and human economic well-being. The Roman Catholic Church has in its papal letters and encyclicals stressed the importance of human solidarity. Francis emphasizes "the intimate relationship between the poor and the fragility of the planet, the conviction that everything in the world is connected, . . . the call to seek other ways of understanding the economy and progress, the value proper to each creature, the human meaning of ecology, . . . the serious responsibility of international and local policy, the throwaway culture, and the proposal of a new lifestyle."[8] He can hardly be clearer in calling all Christians and all people to a recognition of our interdependence in a new economic and environmental situation.

The Cost to Us All

There is a difference between constructive and malicious inequality. Inequality in the service of the common good is not a sin. Indeed, wealth in the service of the common good is estimable. If that inequality and wealth serve the well-being of many, it is admirable. But when our economic system fails to serve the common good and in fact permits suffering, it has become malicious. When underregulated capitalism fails to provide the opportunity for the majority of people to earn the resources to afford a decent life while others benefit disproportionately, it has crossed that line. It has transgressed the contractual terms by which it operates. It no longer serves the common good but promotes an inequality that has neglected many of its citizens, trapping children in poor public schools, resulting in underemployment, and degrading us all. This is not a "soak the rich" book; it does not believe that any simple sort of fix is possible. Instead, it is about making life more fulfilling, more meaningful for all of us. This includes both material sufficiency and also spiritual blossoming. The affluent and the poor are both in distress, however different the two are, because the material poverty of some causes spiritual poverty in us all if we do not take action.

That is why this book is addressed to the whole population, the well-being of the whole, rather than just to the plight of the poor and working poor. Simon Reid-Henry, in his recent book *The Political Origins of Inequality* (2015), suggests the magnitude of the new poverty. He assesses the current situation as the most "unequal and unjust" that the world has ever seen. He writes, "We still have not properly confronted how the poverty and suffering of a great many are connected to the wealth and privilege of a few. We are slow to admit that the problem is one not of poverty traps at the bottom of the pyramid but of a great confinement of wealth at the top."[9] Reid-Henry's analysis is global in scope. My intention here is not to blame the affluent—nor is Reid-Henry's—but to suggest that this interdependent situation is universally destructive of our future.

All of us do better when everyone enjoys a basic level of well-being. Thus, this chapter has focused on our first argument: an ideal state of economic justice would reflect the interdependence of all citizens in our environmental and social life. Though we may not attain this ideal, there is much room for improvement in this area. An improved standard of income stability is a benefit that all Americans need to realize. A more level playing field would make for a healthier society, economically, spiritually, and politically. There is a high cost to the present degree of inequality that characterizes our society.

We turn in the second chapter to a description of what is entailed in human flourishing, what it means to live the good life. This goes beyond survival and entails spiritual well-being;

thus, the chapter considers the spirituality of flourishing. It is concerned with our motivation: the reasons why we care about ALEC. One reason is because we are linked together; our first chapter has demonstrated that. A second reason is spiritual: God has made us family and blesses us with abundant life. When others are not flourishing, we are ourselves lessened. We do, however, seem to have a say in how those blessings are distributed. *Our own flourishing is tied to other people's flourishing.* Our interdependence means that we cannot flourish without others likewise flourishing.

Discussion Questions

1. Prior to reading this chapter, what were your assumptions about asset-limited people, whether above or below the poverty line? What information in this chapter surprised or challenged you?

2. Do you agree with the statement, "If people are working, they shouldn't be poor"? What factors keep people from thriving, even when they are employed?

3. What interconnections do we depend on as a society? How are the poor more vulnerable to broken connections in that web of interdependence?

4. What connections do you depend on for your own financial security? Do you worry about losing any of those connections? Where do you feel the most vulnerable?

5. Compare the stories of Joe and Kathy, both of whom suddenly became homeless. Where do you imagine each of them will be a year later? What advantages and disadvantages do they each have?

6. Why do you think the United States is reluctant to invest the $77 billion the Children's Defense Fund says it would take to reduce childhood poverty by 60 percent?

7. Do you agree there is a "class war" going on? What attitudes about wealth and poverty do you observe in your community? What role does religion play in people's attitudes toward the rich and the poor?

8. What do you consider to be American values? What do you consider to be Christian values? Which of these values complement one another, and which conflict?

9. What is the impact of other people's poverty on your life? Your faith? Your community?

10. How can you learn more about the ALICEs and ALECs in your community? Commit to talking with your neighbors in need before the next session. Ask what their greatest needs are and how your church might help.

CHAPTER 2

TOWARD A SPIRITUALITY
OF FLOURISHING

I volunteer at an agency in Bradenton, Florida, called Turning Points. There, I see a lot of homeless people, a lot of ALICEs, and a lot of people who are temporarily down on their luck. At Turning Points there is a bank of computers designed to help people find work. We have employment counselors present to assist people in doing that. Coming in off the street you can get a haircut, wash your clothes, take a shower, have a meal, apply for food stamps and other benefits, find a food pantry, and even get medical and dental help. I hear some amazing stories of people whose lives have been turned around by the help they find there. Helping others to thrive feels incredibly worthwhile to me. I lose track of time when I work there. My sense is that the other volunteers find it equally worthwhile. This feeds my own soul; it feeds my spirituality. It is not altruistic, nor does it make me feel superior. The sense of flourishing comes from a feeling that what I am doing is worthwhile and contributes to people's well-being.

I should mention that I have been ALEC several times in my life. I can appreciate how easy it is to slip into that income hole and how it feels. I remember it only too well. Everything translated into how much it cost. I felt like many choices were closed to me because I just didn't have the money. I went to a free dental clinic, where my teeth were mangled. Thank goodness I didn't have children then. The experience of having been ALEC myself made me sensitive to the situations of other ALECs, and I know that my own flourishing could not and cannot be complete until their situation is secure.

The new poverty, especially the gap between the working poor and the comfortably fixed, degrades our collective sense of well-being. We may consider ourselves to be flourishing if our own families are safe and well fed, but the truth is we cannot fully flourish when the least among us are not safe and well fed. This is an issue of spirituality. The fact that many people are struggling to get by disrupts our sense of well-being by hinting that our comfortable lifestyles are not built in isolation but may be related to others' struggles. We may not want to hear that, but its impact is still there. When many live in misery or instability, that produces spiritual discomfort for those who are well-off as we seek to justify our comfort and blame the poor for their own condition.

This can lead to distortive and unhealthy spiritual lives. In the face of this inequity, many people live in fear that their own well-being may be threatened, or (possibly as a result of such fear) they adopt a stance of looking after themselves alone, acquiring more and more to add to their comfort. These are two widespread, dangerous reactions to spiritual malaise that we would do well to confront if we want to be spiritually healthy.

Fear: One Response to Economic Insecurity

Henri Nouwen, in his book *Lifesigns*, tells a parable that captures some of the ways being fearful impacts us. Nouwen was writing at a time when nuclear winter was seen as a real possibility. Now terrorist attacks throughout the world are a major source of fear. In this and many other cases, fear has a distortive and reactive effect. Listen to Nouwen's parable about the power of fear:

Once there was a people who surveyed the resources of the world and said to each other: "How can we be sure that we will have enough in hard times? We want to survive whatever happens. Let us start collecting food, materials, and knowledge so that we are safe and secure when a crisis occurs." So they started hoarding, so much and so eagerly that other peoples protested and said, "You have much more than you need, while we don't have enough to survive. Give us part of your wealth!" But the fearful hoarders said: "No, no, we need to keep this in case of an emergency, in case things go bad for us too, in case our lives are threatened." But the others said: "We are dying now, please give us food and materials and knowledge to survive. We can't wait . . . we need it now!"

Then the fearful hoarders became even more fearful, since they became afraid that the poor and hungry would attack them. So they said to one another: "Let us build walls around our wealth so that no stranger can take it from us." They started erecting walls so high that they could not even see anymore whether there were enemies outside the walls or not! As their fear increased they told each other: "Our enemies have become so numerous that they may be able to tear down our walls. Our walls are not strong enough to keep them away. We need to put bombs on top of the walls so that nobody will dare to even come close to us." But instead of feeling safe and secure behind their armed walls they found themselves trapped in the prison they had built with their own fear. They even became afraid of their own bombs, wondering if they might harm themselves more than their enemy. And gradually they realized their fear of death had brought them closer to it.[1]

Even though they had plenty to eat and lived in spacious surroundings, those who built the walls around themselves were spiritually impoverished. We seem to be the people in Nouwen's parable who are dying of fear. This is the opposite of flourishing. Flourishing spiritually involves much more than material well-being.

America has been seen as the "land of opportunity," a place where those who work hard can prosper. It has been assumed that spiritual health might accompany material wealth. However, when material wealth comes at a cost—even if only an indirect and vaguely sensed cost—to others, then it is difficult for us to flourish. This understanding of the good life inevitably if unconsciously undermines our relations with others. Too often the good life means consumption.

Consumerism: Another Response to Insecurity

All of us, the working poor and the comfortable and the wealthy, live in a consumerist culture. This is not a choice that we make, but an undeniable fact; and by consuming we reinforce a pernicious individualism. As theologian Sue McGregor writes, "Consumerism is a way to self-development, self-realization, and self-fulfillment. In a consumer society, an individual's identity is tied to what she or he consumes."[2] This individualistic mind-set unconsciously inhibits our attention to the other. This directly impacts our spirituality.

Our individualism is taught and reinforced by consumerism, which has deep roots in our fear of loss. Consumerism is a false religion, the attractiveness of which lies in the false promise of life's being under our control, training us to put our faith in acquisition, technology, and individual striving. Those values are raised to a level of transcendence that escapes challenge. Both rich and poor live under the illusion that happiness lies just beyond the next purchase. The wealthy are envied because they appear to have significant choices and control; the poor believe that their unhappiness will be relieved through access to the exercise of choice. To ALICE the wealthy appear to be comfortable enough to enjoy their lives and to be spiritually healthy.

There is a myth that if one works hard, then one will "make it" in America, "making it" being defined as success and financial security. While being successful is no substitute for spiritual flourishing, it is also true that hardworking ALECs who believe in hard work and yet do *not* realize an increased sense of security are left wondering what went wrong. Many develop a deep resentment alongside a sense of entitlement. That feeling of being duped by the system seems understandable for the working poor but not for the comfortably fixed, who wonder why, having worked hard *and* achieved success, they are not any more satisfied spiritually. Consumerism is an especially deep-rooted and pernicious disease for the affluent because their freedom to consume can be taken as a substitute for interdependence. Their own limitedness and dependence can more easily be disguised for them. Thus even wealth, if it is not appreciated or shared with other people, will not lead to joy.[3]

The confrontation with our malaise points to our need for a spiritual renewal, retraining our focus on gratitude and the common good. Sometimes our consumerism is brought up short by encountering an example of generosity and forgiveness. Consider this story, for example:

> Sarasota's Joshua and Hannah Morris decided it was better to do good in the world after their bicycles went missing from their garage in Sarasota Springs. They found their bikes four streets over in a neighbor's yard. The 30-year-old Morris did not press charges after he called authorities to come and retrieve the items.
>
> Then Morris and his wife decided to buy $166 worth of groceries and a brand new bike for the couple and their son who had stolen the bikes. The man told Morris that it was his mother's house and he had received an eviction notice. "I knew they had a rough situation going on," Morris said. "I felt it was the right thing to do. I had my 10-month-old son, Levi, there with me and there is

a lot of negativity in the world. I wasn't looking for recognition. I wanted Levi to know if you can't find good in the world, you can make it yourself."

Morris said the incident reminded him of Luke 6:28, which reads, "Bless those who curse you. Pray for those who mistreat you." The neighbors reacted with shock when the Morrises, who attend Bayside Community Church, showed up with packages. "They were extremely grateful and in tears," said Morris.[4]

This story illustrates for me the power of not living by individual consumerism. The Morrises seem to be spiritually healthy people. Clearly we can only speculate on the other family's reaction to the Morrises' not retaliating but instead trying to help the family. This story illustrates for me the power of not living by individual consumerism. The Morrises seem to be spiritually healthy people, prioritizing grace and generosity over personal property. This is not a new temptation: as Jesus put it, "No slave can serve two masters. . . . You cannot serve God and wealth" (Luke 16:13). I do not think Jesus was making a political or social statement here but rather a spiritual one. What has priority in our lives? We often feel that "God helps those who help themselves" and that we must look after ourselves. However, serving the master of self leaves us feeling isolated and unhappy; if we are to follow God, we learn to share and find that, rather than being diminished, we are strengthened by this sharing. In fact, it may not be too much to say that as we look after others, we find ourselves looked after. If we are healthy, we open ourselves to others, we see how much we receive from others and also how much we can give them. Relationships with others are fundamental to our well-being and at the core of our joy and flourishing.

Christians, and American Christians in particular, tend to put a high value on flourishing; indeed, if there be such a thing, this is part of American spirituality. Too often we equate flourishing with consuming, and consuming is an individual pursuit. The understanding that human beings were designed to flourish is also part of most religious traditions; however, they may flesh out what that involves differently than we do. This book is based on specifically Christian beliefs, so this chapter will address two questions about flourishing from a Christian perspective: First, what constitutes flourishing? And second, what can motivate us to enlarge our own flourishing and promote the flourishing of others? We take up those two questions in turn.

What Constitutes Flourishing?

Since our view of flourishing may be distorted by the two responses just explored—fear and consumerism—it is necessary for us to consider what exactly is involved in genuine flourishing. After all, it is our pursuit of the good life that has propelled us into a false spirituality. I would add that there is much that is right and necessary in our vision, but that only makes the rooting out of the distortions harder. We have to get our vision straight before we can say how we can correct the spiritual malaise we experience. So what exactly is necessary to flourishing? One thing is a basic level of material security.

Americans value work, and contributing to one's own and the public's well-being, and freedom of opportunity; these all point to and rest on the creation of a society where all people have access to a decent standard of living. Many of our values center on being meaningfully employed in a system that makes use of the skills we can contribute. The bedrock for flourishing is having the necessities of life, including food, shelter, and companionship, along with security from immediate threat.

One of my graduate school friends, Ed Loring, started a house of hospitality in Atlanta after having taught at Columbia Seminary and served as pastor of a local Presbyterian church. The Open Door Community, a Christ-centered residential community and political action group, began out of that church. The home consists of middle-class resident volunteers and people in need. Those off the street contribute their work toward community tasks. People eat together; as Ed says, "Justice is important, but supper is essential." Murphy Davis, the cofounder of Open Door and its prison ministry director, takes pains to assert that the ministry of justice is not diminished by attention to this most basic need. "Without supper, without love, without table companionship, justice can become a program that we do to people," Murphy told Christine Pohl, as recounted in Pohl's book *Making Room: Recovering Hospitality as a Christian Tradition.*[5]

A second broad element of flourishing has to do with realizing our value as human beings. Every person is loved by God, and God yearns for our love in return. Thus each person is intrinsically valuable. Each also has God-given gifts that can be offered up to God to be used to fulfill God's purposes. We can each affirm our value and respect our basic God-given worth. We can flourish on the basis of God's love if we realize that we are valuable. It is important to respect our own gifts and also to affirm those of others. We come to self-respect by being affirmed and respected. The brokenness of many ALICEs and ALECs is that they do not respect themselves; a community communicating respect can offer the working poor a chance to see themselves in a light that does not equate worth with income. This suggests that we all have the ability to contribute, that in fact we all have value; this can issue in a basic hopefulness about life. The future can be seen as open, rather than closed, as being as much communal as individual.

Being treated with basic justice or fairness is a third element of flourishing. Fair treatment reinforces respect and indicates that these elements of flourishing are syncretistic. Justice is the notion that people should be treated with equal respect or regard. This is especially important in regard to racial justice. To discriminate against anyone on the basis of their social group is to reject the goal of equal treatment and to attempt to justify unjust distribution of wealth, position, and other attributes. A sense of deprivation can give rise to resentment and crime, and the blissful ignorance of the privileged leads to callousness and protectionism that ignores the realities of the working poor's situations. Treating others unfairly detracts from our own flourishing.

Linking the topics of what constitutes flourishing and what might motivate us to seek others' flourishing and our own is the fourth and most important aspect of flourishing: *shalom*, or the vision of a loving, joyful, mutual community. The design of creation was such that every part of creation was interrelated in a harmonious whole. This same *shalom* was one that Jesus Christ revealed in his desire that all creation flourish and be made whole. It is virtually impossible to imagine that we could flourish in the absence of community. Social connection is so much at the heart of us that we wither in the absence of mutuality; it is worth noting that the epidemic of Columbine-type shootings were almost invariably committed by isolated individuals lacking community. *Shalom* is the solidarity that all creatures share with each other, which is often broken but nevertheless remains interrelated despite brokenness. It is characterized by contentment, peace, and joy.

This description of flourishing has the power to uncover the false promises of self-involved fear and consumerism. It suggests the reason why those are false paths — namely, that they elevate one's own well-being far above that of others. The resulting isolation and divisiveness are themselves the sources of our malaise. Rather than cooperate with each other and love the neighbor, we compete by loving only the self. In Christian terms, we think of Paul's assertion in 1 Corinthians 12 that all are members of one body, but if some parts of the body act as though they are better than others, or do not recognize their dependence on others, then we break the bond of interrelatedness that is at the heart of flourishing.

What Motivates People to Work for Flourishing?

We have seen what blocks flourishing; we now turn to the question of what could motivate our development of a spirituality of flourishing. We have known people who we felt were flourishing. They seem, no matter what their material circumstances, to be centered and serene. They are, in fact, so secure in their own joy that they share easily and are able to encourage the material and spiritual flourishing of others. This is an essential step toward living out our own mission to serve those in need.

"Kathy," from Hope Family Services, a domestic violence center in Bradenton, is one such person who has discovered what it takes to flourish:

"My mother was married to a very abusive alcoholic. He would go on binges and beat her. My first memories of Christmas were of me and my mom hiding behind the water heater in the basement. We were running away from my stepfather, who was in a drunken stupor upstairs. . . . I was around 6 years old, and all I remember thinking was, 'Santa won't find me here.' When you have lived in that kind of environment as a child, it sticks with you. I'm very grateful that my life has turned around and I was very fortunate my mother survived: that's one of the reasons why I try to help other people.

"I've volunteered at HOPE for 12 years. When anyone walks in the door—whether they're a volunteer or a client— they're treated with such respect. You get the sense that you're in a place that's protected and you'll get the help you need."[6]

In Kathy's comments you can see elements that enabled her to transform her life: a confrontation with abuse; finding a community of others seeking to flourish; developing a sense of purpose and gratitude; and, I suspect, though it's not said, a relationship with a higher power, God.

Theologian Dawn Nothwehr has explored the question of how spiritual transformation happens, how struggling people become peaceful, other-regarding people. Kathy's story reflects the key elements that Nothwehr identifies as being involved in our transformation toward flourishing: (1) recognition and confrontation of spiritual malaise; (2) participation in supportive communities that boost our search for a deeper spirituality; (3) gratitude, which can generate an acceptance even of death and suffering as involved in flourishing and joy; and (4) identification with God.[7] We have already discussed in this chapter how confronting our spiritual malaise means repenting of our typical coping mechanisms—fear and consumerism. Let's examine the other elements of transformation she describes and how they can motivate us to work toward greater flourishing for all.

Supportive community. Nothwehr has found that participation in groups that foster our search for a deeper spirituality is essential to transformation. Two things that are vital to flourishing happen in support groups: we must make ourselves vulnerable to those whom we trust will maintain our confidentiality and continue to relate to us, and others must make themselves vulnerable to us. In sharing with each other we take the risk of being ourselves and finding that this is OK, that we can be cared for—even loved—despite our warts and flaws being visible. We learn that caring for others also involves taking steps to make sure that they can enjoy a decent quality of life. The spiritual and the material interpenetrate. We can ourselves accept aid from others. Thus we learn that others care for us and that we can care for them, in concrete ways as well as relational ones. Churches can be great places to give birth to support groups like Bible studies, twelve-step groups, book clubs, and long-term friendships.

Generosity and gratitude. In their recent book *The Paradox of Generosity,* Christian Smith and Hilary Davidson define generosity as "the virtue of giving good things to others freely and abundantly."[8] They found that generosity—giving money, volunteering, being relationally generous, being an authentic neighbor and friend—is positively associated with greater personal happiness, physical health, and growth in well-being. Having a stronger sense of purpose in life is also part of this. In our focus on flourishing, we can quote their summary: "Generosity tends to nurture love in the giver, and love stands at the heart of human flourishing, so generosity naturally tends to promote human flourishing."[9]

Gratitude—a recognition that one has been graced beyond what one is owed—seems to arise spontaneously in those moments when we are overwhelmed with beauty or the generosity of others. Rather than assuming that some people are naturally thankful and others more reserved or even bitter, *Washington Post* columnist E. J. Dionne argues that gratitude is a discipline. As a disposition, a virtue, and a way of thinking all at once, Dionne suggests that gratitude can be learned.[10] True thanksgiving begins with humility, the humility to recognize that we did not create ourselves, and that everything we have or are is a gift.

Generosity and gratitude may also contribute to an acceptance of suffering and death as part of a contented, flourishing life, or at least not cause for despair. The world today seems full of terror and threats. It is hard for us to imagine joy as an actuality rather than an illusion that we have to force ourselves to swallow or pretend to swallow. It is hard to feel joyous and to flourish in the face of today's realities. On the other hand, we are told that the world is in God's hands. Suffering is not illusory; the attacks in San Bernardino, Paris, Orlando, and Nice really happened. Beneath those tragedies, however, the Christian believes that there can be real joy and flourishing. God suffered, died, and rose from the dead in order to indicate that joy and love are far more powerful than suffering and death. God does everything he can to reveal that death does not have the final word. In fact, Christians affirm that suffering and death have been overcome by the joy and flourishing of the resurrection.

Identification with God. By including "identification of the Source of Life" as one of the elements motivating people toward flourishing, Nothwehr is pointing toward a sense that our lives are suffused with a higher purpose, a sense that we are doing the will of God. Those who are flourishing, who feel a sense of purpose in their lives, are not living fearful or consumer-oriented existences. Perhaps it is this that enables Christians to accept death and suffering as part of joy and flourishing, that gives them a sense that living generously is its own reward and a trust that God will in fact keep us in his care. This trust frees us to live in harmony with God, nature, and others. We can offer our lives to God, to use the powers we have been given for the sake of the whole earth community.

Building on the transformative spirituality we have described in this chapter, we desire to be formed into people who are generous, who care, who are grateful, and who live out that gratitude. Martin Copenhaver, a wise pastor, suggests that we "give and spend where we want our hearts to be, and then let [our] hearts catch up."[11] If we put our treasure where we want our hearts to be, then our hearts will follow. He is advising us to act thankfully, whether we feel it at first or not. "So," writes Copenhaver, "sometimes, especially at first, we don't come to worship to offer our thanks to God because we are thankful. Rather we come to worship to offer our thanks so that one day we shall be thankful."[12]

Practicing generosity of time, money, and concern also has a spiraling effect; it builds the generosity of those who engage in such practices. These are ways of growing in compassion, entering into the lives of others and the ways in which they enrich our own. The perception that we can experience what the other is going through is at the heart of solidarity. Compassion establishes a linkage, a fellowship. It is this feeling of expansiveness that reinforces our compassion and brings us to flourishing. The practice of compassion—literally, "suffering with"—expands into a solidarity with others in the recognition that flourishing is the intention of the Creator for all peoples. As Henri Nouwen writes, "All Christian action . . . is a manifestation of the human solidarity revealed to us in the house of God. It is not an anxious human effort to create a better world. It is a confident expression of the truth that in Christ, death, evil, and destruction have been overcome."[13]

While you may be eager to jump into the strategies for addressing economic inequality, chapters 1 and 2 have been intended to lay the spiritual groundwork for the work you hope to do in your community. Efforts to "serve the poor" will fall flat without a true understanding of the interconnectedness of human flourishing. Concern for others' flourishing is an element of our own flourishing; it does not detract from it. The Christian theological vision of *shalom*, and Jesus' command that we are to love our neighbor as ourselves, emphasize that in fact loving the neighbor is an integral way of loving God. And that is what lies at the heart of our own joy and flourishing. This is true for both ALEC and the affluent, of course. We are each to work toward living into the realization that the other's flourishing is interdependent with our own.

The reciprocity of flourishing is one that we have to learn. The well-off must learn what it means to be generous without being patronizing or paternalistic. On the other hand, ALICE and ALEC must sense that they have something to offer to the flourishing of the well-off. There is much to learn in this regard. What is quite clear is that we must act, and act wisely. We must be interested not just in good intentions but in the *effectiveness* of programs designed to promote the flourishing of others. We now turn to the investigation of programs that are effective.

Discussion Questions

1. In what ways are material flourishing and spiritual flourishing related? How is your spirituality affected by your material circumstances? How is your spirituality affected by someone else's material needs?

2. Of what are you afraid? What is the deepest fear of which you are conscious? Is that fear justified?

3. How does consumerism affect you? To what degree does it matter to you that you are able to have what you want? Are you envious of something that others have? Do you find that "things" can interfere with your relationships with others?

4. How would you define the good life? According to the criteria discussed in this chapter — material needs being met, feeling valued as a human being, being treated justly and fairly, and experiencing *shalom* in loving community — do you feel you are truly flourishing? Are others in your community?

5. How is God related to our flourishing? When has the church communicated respect and care for you? What other communities of mutuality have communicated this element?

6. What motivates you and your church or organization to work for the flourishing of all people? Do the elements described in the chapter—confronting spiritual malaise, finding a group for support, practicing generosity, and experiencing God's call and guidance—seem appropriate to your community? Would you say that you experience all four?

7. How might our transformation into grateful and generous people begin? What actions could you take to better integrate spiritual and material flourishing in your context?

CHAPTER 3

STRATEGY 1: RELIEF

At the same time that we realize our own joy and flourishing is interdependent with that of others, we may feel crushed by the reality of so many people experiencing a declining quality of life. We ourselves may be ALICE; surely some of our friends, acquaintances, and fellow parishioners are. In this situation it is essential to recognize that as individuals or as groups we can make a difference. That difference is almost always more than just a sense of empowerment for ourselves, but our own empowerment is in itself very important. We can act to improve others' quality of life and thus improve our own.

We can promote a good quality of life for every American by using four strategies or approaches. Not every citizen will participate on all four levels; nevertheless, achieving the vision of economic well-being for all will entail adequate action on all four: charity or almsgiving, personal and neighborhood self-help, creation of an ethos for action through cultural opinion formation, and governmental or policy action.

Relief, also called charity or almsgiving, can clearly be a strategy of groups as well as of individuals as we provide goods or services to people in desperate situations. While it should not be our only strategy for addressing economic injustice in our communities, relief of poverty's symptoms nonetheless has an appropriate role in addressing distress. It is important to recognize, even though we will look at the underside of charity in this chapter and see in subsequent chapters how other strategies address inequality on a systemic level, that there are innumerable stories of food banks, clothes closets, and spiritual counseling that meet immediate needs in an exemplary way. Food ministries, health ministries, denominational disaster relief offices, the Red Cross and Red Crescent organizations, the CARE program, Oxfam, and more are on the front lines, serving people in desperate situations.

Relieving ALICE's Distress

Each of us probably has acted and continues to act as an individual to address someone's need. You have handed a dollar bill to a man or woman on the street or helped someone out of a desperate dilemma or contributed to a charity. It would be surprising if you did not receive five or six solicitations a week from various agencies. You find some of these appealing and may even contribute to one or two of them. Regularly our churches announce a special offering for the victims of hurricanes in Haiti or earthquakes in Guatemala or typhoons in the Philippines. As I write, many areas of Texas and Oklahoma have been devastated by floods and are generating similar responses.

In many cases working people who are not earning a comfortable income run into trouble. A catastrophic event happens and they are unable to continue working. Because they live on such a tight income margin, the working poor may be hit especially hard by such an incident. They may have to find another house or apartment to rent or even live out of their car. They may have to move in with a relative or friend. If they are fortunate, they may be able to get a loan to tide them over.[1] If the catastrophe is losing employment, that is a double whammy. First and obviously, it throws into doubt one's ability to afford future spending. Second, however, is the damage that this does to one's psyche or soul, especially in the United States, where one's status is connected with one's job. The most pernicious aspect of this is that one begins to believe that the loss of the job was due to one's own incompetence or lack of responsibility rather than seeing it as a result at least partially of social structural factors. (This varies by incident, of course.) While outwardly one can complain about the stupidity or ignorance of the boss, inwardly there are few who can avoid the psychological impact of that loss. Finding a job with comparable pay and benefits after having been let go can be difficult.

There is, to be sure, a network of agencies designed to help address this situation. Organizations may offer computer access to search for jobs online and assist people in scanning employment announcements. Networking with friends and acquaintances may turn up something. Retraining centers may be able to help people retool for another job. Housing services and agencies can be tapped. There is the possibility of unemployment compensation, indigent hospital care, supplemental food stamps, pro bono legal representation, and other services meant to allow ALICE to find a decent living situation. In all of these there is an aspect of relief, a strategy designed for short-term assistance.

We suspect that readers will be able to name any number of agencies or organizations that provide relief in their community. Without the efforts of charitable organizations and individuals, there would be far less hope for ALICE as well as for the poor. Many of these agencies are staffed by ALECs for other ALECs. There are food pantries that distribute emergency food and offer other forms of temporary assistance. Relief is an important strategy when the immediate situation calls for remediation, for meeting all those needs that, if unmet, would result in terrible consequences. Relief fills a vital niche in the network of care that enables all citizens to live beyond disaster.

The Ambiguity of Charity

There is much to commend social agency services and charity in general, but we must note that there is a pejorative nuance to the word "charity." Charity carries the connotation of dependency, giving to recipients without expectation of reciprocity. There are clearly situations in which the victims of circumstance or natural disasters are in dire need of charity or relief. Little is expected of the recipients because they are not able to take care of themselves and thus not able to reciprocate. Relief is, ideally, provided only so long as persons are unable to help themselves. Indeed, this should shape the way relief is conducted from the outset.

There are definitely occasions when this kind of relief is appropriate and commendable. When the situation is urgent and the temporary provision of emergency aid to reduce immediate suffering from a damaging human crisis or a natural one is vital, then relief is commendable. There is a need to stop the bleeding, either literal or figurative. The Good Samaritan's bandaging of the man who fell among robbers is such an occasion.

However, there are other occasions when the provision of relief generates more damage than it alleviates. If what began as temporary charity or welfare continues even after the situation is no longer immediately threatening a person or family, then charity can begin to cause people's skills and abilities to care for themselves to dry up. Charity can take the place of our normal expectation that people will be able to take care of themselves. Sustained charity, when the emergency has passed, can create dependency.

When an individual or group makes the commitment to provide charity or relief, such work needs to recognize the interdependence of giver and receiver. Relief should be provided in such a way as to foster interdependence and respect the immediate needs and beliefs of the receiver. This respect and recognition of the humanity of the receiver is essential to the effectiveness and long-term impact of relief.

Consider the following example:

Since 2007 there has been an increase nationwide in food insecurity—not being able to afford proper meals. While there are food pantries and other feeding ministries run by churches, there is a particular wrinkle here in my area of Florida, where the economy booms for just a few months a year as vacationers from around the country come to the beach for spring break. When the spring vacation season ends and tourism wanes because of the summer heat, there is a decline in the need for tourism-related work. Some people lose their jobs; some have their hours cut back.

The summer months deliver a double whammy to low-income families. Half of the children in Sarasota County schools qualify for free or reduced-cost lunch at school during the school year. When schools are closed for the summer, families must provide these meals at the same time their household income is reduced. In response to this problem, All Faiths Food Bank created the Campaign Against Summer Hunger, which provided more than 1.5 million meals in Sarasota and DeSoto Counties in 2014. As commendable as that and similar programs are, providing food does not solve the problem. Stable jobs and decent housing are also essential.

A study of ALICE conducted by the United Way of Florida found that 45 percent of Florida households struggle to pay for household necessities, says Lars Gilberts, United Way executive director for ALICE follow-up in Florida. For families with food insecurity, a car breaking down or a change in work schedule can affect their ability to afford food.

The meeting of immediate needs by food-bank programs is not an end unto itself but a stopgap that helps families focus on their own long-term solutions. "That bag of food is not all about hunger. It's about keeping their job, keeping their home," says Gilberts.[2]

The danger of charity is not so much financial as spiritual. People begin to think of themselves as "welfare cases." Part of the reason is that victims of job loss, housing loss, or natural disasters have more than physical needs. They are related to

God spiritually, to themselves emotionally, to others socially, and to the rest of creation wholistically. Thus, for example, in times of need they may see themselves as being punished by God; they may have low self-confidence, may feel inferior to others, and may think nature has dealt them an extra low blow. Ministering to physical needs is sometimes done in such a way as to ignore those other aspects of ourselves, constituting only emergency first aid without recognition of the range of full, embodied persons. Just because people are in difficult or life-threatening circumstances does not render other, relational aspects of who they are any less real. Those other aspects of the self may be suppressed to the external observer who is providing relief, but they are very much alive in the recipient. Thus the manner in which relief is provided becomes quite significant.

Steve Corbett, a community development expert, sees the way in which charity can be harmful as well as helpful. Those who dispense charity need to see the recipients as full human beings and themselves as not superior to or beyond the situation of those they are helping. He puts it this way: "Until we embrace our mutual brokenness, our work with low-income people is liable to do more harm than good."[3] Until help givers understand that they have the same makeup (spiritual, emotional, social, and ecological) as those they seek to help, their work may well be paternalistic, condescending, and damaging. ALICEs often already see themselves as somewhat inferior to others, and the superior or pitying way those who are providing relief may do so can worsen that sense of inability. Taken to an extreme or for long periods of time, this may immobilize the working poor from taking initiative.

Charity accompanied by an attitude of being mutually broken and coming alongside the recipient of charity can help in restoring a sense of self-worth. It recognizes that relief is only temporary and seeks to restore people to a sense of their full relational self so that they can support themselves; its goal is to encourage those in dire straits to reach a point where they can seek to glorify God by working to support themselves and their families through their vocations. Thus this approach to caring can encourage recipients to earn a living through their own efforts and to gain a sense of their worth. It may be motivated by a sense of humility or a desire to help someone else as we have been helped in the past. At its best, charity can begin to create a sense of relationship with others. It recognizes that we are all related to each other. This consideration begins to show us the necessity of the second of our four approaches, self-help—participation in improving one's own life, which will be discussed in the next chapter.

Doing Relief Well

We have been looking at situations where charity was essential and timely, helping to restore victims of loss to self-support and healthy lifestyles. As we have said, however, helping can be harmful, even with the best of intentions. Let's examine how churches and other organizations can do relief work well and not so well in three contexts: ongoing, local relief efforts; short-term mission trips; and disaster response.

Ongoing Relief
The first is the sort of relief that can be easily imagined and implemented by local churches and other organizations, responding to life-threatening situations like hunger, illness, and exposure to the elements.

A recent example involved a case of financial instability that had snowballed into a family's potential devastation: A homeless family of five approached Turning Points with no money and no way of meeting their immediate needs. While the husband and wife had some job skills, they had needs that could not wait until they found employment. Turning Points was able to secure some motel housing at a reduced cost subsidized by the agency itself. To meet their needs for clothing and food, one of the Turning Points volunteers swung into action. He asked twelve families in Peace Presbyterian Church to each take a dinner to the family in the motel. During the next two weeks the husband and the wife found jobs, the kids were enrolled in schools, and the future, which had seemed so bleak before, had begun to brighten considerably. The gift of those two weeks gave the family enough stability to find jobs, settle children, and find housing for themselves. This is invaluable relief which offers a cushion of continuity in emergency situations.

Joe, the builder and tile worker we met in chapter 1, had been gut-punched by the property owner demanding back rent and then by the totaling of his truck. His family was rendered homeless. The rest of the story is that a churchman heard of Joe's situation and found a way to house Joe and his family in temporary quarters and help Joe get another truck. Joe got back on his feet and found a home for his family. Others in the provider's church contributed as well. This is also a good example of relief.

One of my favorite examples of church-based relief is an organization in my area called the Foods Resource Bank, which links up urban and rural churches. The FRB is designed to relieve hunger by enabling churches to work together to produce a crop, sell it, and then send the proceeds to a denominational hunger program, a global project, or one of the FRB projects for the self-development of people. By providing money and other resources, the urban church enables a farmer or group of farmers at a rural church to grow a crop and sell it on the market. At the end of harvest there is a festival at which urban and rural peoples celebrate the crop. Besides the relief aspect of this work, the FRB has also helped revitalize a number of churches.

Churches and other organizations do this sort of relief regularly, for example, through food pantries, the support of emergency shelters for abused women, the subsidization of decent housing for a limited period of time, volunteer tax preparation, parish health ministry, and halfway houses. One frequently unmet need is for mental health services. Note that all of these examples address emergency situations, offer temporary relief, and are vital to the well-being of individuals. However, some thought needs to be given to assisting recipients in making the transition to independent living, at best, and at least to some semi-independent or assisted living. While churches might offer meals or emergency shelter on a weekly basis, ideally the clientele will rotate as other strategies help struggling people gain stability enough to avoid life-threatening conditions that need immediate relief.

Short-Term Missions

Many churches organize short-term missions (STMs) to provide relief work in impoverished communities or areas stricken by natural disasters. Often the work involves building houses or churches, conducting vacation Bible schools, doing neighborhood rehabilitation, and other charity projects overseas or in the United States. The terms of these projects range from three or four days to two weeks. Ideally, these trips involve emergency relief or other necessary work that local people, for whatever reason, are unable to do for themselves.

Youth groups often do short-term work in relief agencies that provide vital breaks for the often-fatigued caregivers. One church provided a week of rest for those who were cooking and serving meals to the homeless. Another did housing repairs for those who cannot do that for themselves—and has been doing that sort of work for years.

While STMs are well-intentioned, their impact may be more stimulating for the givers than the receivers. Their value for the population being served depends largely on the amount of preparation and debriefing that goes on for the workers before the trip, emphasizing sensitivity and awareness of the cultures they are working in. The value depends on how committed charity providers are to establishing relationships with the recipients, how fully they recognize the personhood of those they are working for. In the ideal case, the group spends three or four sessions studying just what is involved in the community they will work in and how their own participation can be meaningful to them and not only a short-term fix. They consider how their efforts are faith based and put a human face on charity. Often friendships develop between local people and the short-term men and women, boys and girls.

Several qualities of the trip will determine its success. The serving groups must become aware of their own cultural biases and those of the receiving group. This step is both vital and complex. Cultures differ in their concept of self: Is the self more individual, as those in the West conceive themselves, or do people tend to think of themselves collectively or in terms of the family? Many U.S. and U.K. organizations tend to be task-oriented and functional in orientation. Being aggressive and task-oriented ("Get 'er done!"), people from a Western or urban cultural milieu are often anxious to get to work. They have, after all, come all this way and are ready to work. Their greater affluence also may influence the way they see less well-fixed communities and individuals, so they may see ALECs as deficient or incompetent in some ways. They often override local norms and fail to incorporate the values and customs of the receiving group. "If they were able to take care of themselves they would not be in this jam," may be the subconscious attitude of the mission team members.

To sum up the effect of some of these cultural biases, it may be that the people in the location receiving help are not consulted about whether they want help and what help they may want. Did members of the receiving community or group participate in assessing, designing, implementing, monitoring, and evaluating the assistance program? Were they involved in deciding on the nature of the response? For example, some houses may have been painted by the STM volunteers when they could have been painted by the residents. Is assistance based on vulnerability and need, and appropriately and equitably directed? Did the aid workers demonstrate appropriate attitudes? And, perhaps most important, will this work be sustainable once the short-term missioners leave? How will the community be impacted by the work done? All these questions go well beyond the casual, if not cavalier, attitude that some relief workers take toward the people being cared for. The most helpful STMs partner with local people and address the issues described in such a way that the receiving community is able to build on the genuine help that is offered.

Some not-so-subliminal messages are communicated when the aid team simply assumes on the basis of the opinion of one local leader what their primary task or objective should be. The leader may believe that the monetary donations given by the group are so essential that the local community ought to simply agree without question when the aid organization proposes certain projects. Though those projects may be unnecessary or even detrimental, the leadership cannot afford to offend the people who are making essential monetary donations to the community.

Sometimes the well-heeled bring with them expensive electric tools or electronic devices that far outshine local capacities. The group might make sure that any equipment that is left can be repaired by local people. The quality or speed of the work the STM does may outstrip that of local workers and resources, and may leave the home group feeling inferior or incapable. Short-term work enables groups to do their best labor because it is limited to a short time. The worse consequence may be that the home group simply capitulates to the expertise of the outsiders, as well-intentioned as the aid providers may be, and come to consider themselves incapable of assisting themselves. "We will just let others take care of us," may be the unspoken subtext.

In short, there are hidden potholes in the assistance road. ALICEs who are discouraged may rely on outside, state, or government aid to get them back on their feet. Relief efforts, to put it baldly, should be implemented only in urgent, life-threatening situations. And, even then, they should enlist the participation of the people being assisted to the maximum extent possible. They need to respect the dignity of the people receiving aid. The object is to encourage people to support themselves and their families to the enrichment of community and the glory of God. Self-development should be one of the objectives of relief from the outset.

Disaster Response
Natural disasters are the quintessential example of when relief is the most appropriate strategy. Disasters leave people homeless and jobless—ALICEs and ALECs, if even for a short time.

People empathize with the plight of those in the affected area, and there is often an overwhelming response of people who want to help relieve the suffering. Some short-term mission teams respond to natural disasters, both in the United States and around the world. Sometimes STMs are quite capable of providing disaster assistance, or it may be more effective to offer financial support to relief agencies best equipped to do the work. Sometimes front-line physical labor is needed, performed by groups doing STMs or by larger agencies with a long-term presence in the area; sometimes the need is for direct support for those who are financially strapped; sometimes it is financial support for those who are seeking to rehabilitate devastated neighborhoods. Some research may be needed to find the most trustworthy agency, through rating services like Charity Navigator, Charity Watch, or Give Well. Disaster situations call for a response of relief, but as with ongoing efforts and STMs, there are right and wrong ways to respond.

On November 8, 2013, the super typhoon Yolanda hit the large city of Tacloban, Philippines (pop. 225,000), and the entire coastline area and towns of eastern Leyte Island with a force that killed thousands and devastated the landscape. (The government stopped counting at 6,500 dead, and many are still missing.) Its impact could be considered equivalent in destruction to the Katrina and Sandy hurricanes or the tornadoes that hit Joplin, Missouri, and Greensburg, Kansas. It was more catastrophic in terms of the number of people killed and the sheer range of calamity it brought. Furthermore, the region is relatively remote from the largest cities and centers of aid, and the infrastructure needed to transport aid (such as roads and airports) was severely damaged.

Karl M. Gaspar, CSsR, a Redemptorist priest in the Philippines, did a concrete ethnographic and sociotheological report of the response to this typhoon.[4] When Gaspar arrived at Tacloban City a month after the typhoon struck, he found many aid agencies working to relieve the hunger resulting from the disaster but inadvertently adding to the crisis by occupying many of the usable resources—transport, boardinghouses, hotels, and surviving buildings—in this very poor region. There was very little coordination of the effort to bring relief to the Waray people among the aid agencies and none by the government for ten months. There was also no system of accounting for the distribution of monetary aid. Instead, Gaspar emphasizes the phenomenon of "turfing" (fighting for influence) among aid agencies and the government:

> There is also the whole politics of aid where protecting turf, projecting their own accomplishments to their constituencies to secure more funding, favoring the competence of foreigners while negating the local staff's experience and the tendency to operate as lone wolves have blocked the needed collaboration among various humanitarian agencies at work in Tacloban. With very limited coordination among them, there has not been a clearing house which would prevent duplication of efforts and inequitable distribution of relief goods such that some villages get the bulk of the goods while others—especially in the interior and the margins—get nothing.[5]

Noticeable in this assessment are (1) the way aid agencies respond to their institutional constituencies and act to reward their own systems, even in the midst of disasters; (2) the tendency to discount local knowledge and to valorize the technical and scientific perspectives brought by outsiders; and (3) the way that lack of coordination results in unfair distribution of food, ignoring some populations while distributing goods to the more conveniently located proximate communities.

As can happen in STM relief efforts, technical solutions overrode the cultural norms and beliefs of the local people in the Philippines. Local citizens were not engaged to participate in determining the shape that rehabilitation was to take. As Gaspar writes, "When disaster agencies and governments take the grassroots people for granted and monopolize the processes in DRRM (Disaster Risk Reduction and Management), human agency is not empowered and tends to disappear."[6] The "victims"

Resources for Relief

Often there is no need for churches to reinvent the wheel by starting their own ministries to address a certain community need. Established ministries and nonprofit organizations are generally happy to partner with groups and individuals who want to support and participate in their work. The following Web sites can help you find agencies with whom you might partner.

Feeding America supports thousands of food banks and feeding programs nationwide. Use their site to find local options for involvement. www.feedingamerica.org/find-your-local-foodbank

The **Foods Resource Bank** links rural church people who have land, labor, and know-how with urban congregations who can support and learn from producers. www.foodsresourcebank.org

Your community probably has more programs for the homeless than you realize. Use **Homeless Shelter Directory** to find shelters and services in your area. www.homelessshelterdirectory.org

Your denomination's mission office might be a good starting point for coordinating short-term mission trips. The **Presbyterian Mission Agency** has many resources for planning a trip that will help and not hurt. www.presbyterianmission.org/ministries/world-mission/missiontrips/

Denominations' disaster assistance programs often offer tangible ways for churches to get involved by assembling supply kits, hosting volunteer work teams, and so on:

— Presbyterian Church (USA) Disaster Assistance, http://pda.pcusa.org
— United Methodist Committee on Relief, http://www.umcor.org
— Episcopal Relief and Development, http:// www.episcopalrelief.org
— United Church of Christ Disaster Ministries, http://www.ucc.org/oghs/national/
— Global Ministries, a partnership of the Christian Church (Disciples of Christ) and the United Church of Christ, http://www.globalministries.org

felt powerless in the face of their diminishment. The ignorance of the aid providers concerning the beliefs of the Waray people resulted in their burying the dead in mass graves rather than permitting the Waray to identify and bury their dead in a religious ceremony. Such insensitivity haunted the survivors, who consider it an egregious violation not to identify and bury the dead with dignity. Violating this taboo may well be the result of ignorance not just of local cultural values but also of the spiritual aspects of suffering and pain. The aid providers may not have the sensitivity to recognize people's broken hearts or grief. They may be unaware of the emotional power that loss and failure bring to those who are threatened with death or who experience the deaths of loved ones. The notion that we are all broken and all vulnerable, if it were to penetrate the psyches and structures of the aid providers, would transform their work. It would mean that the aid workers could see that the disaster or loss was a spiritual crisis.

This is not to say all responses were done poorly; there were also examples of a quite sensitive recognition of the constitution and beliefs of local Catholics and also collaborative work to rebuild livelihood-generating businesses. Gaspar's group, the Redemptorist Fathers in the Philippines, along with other indigenous priests and missioners, brought local sensibilities and were aware that the typhoon represented a blow to people's faith. The priests understood the importance of listening to the people affected by disaster. The immediate need after the typhoon for affected people was to make meaning of this trauma. They needed people to listen to them as they told their stories over and over in order to wrest theological meaning from the catastrophe. The dominant image of God was of one who protected them from harm, a God who gifted them with a second life and who provided for their needs when the going got very rough during and after Yolanda. There was a sense that this God was also vulnerable and suffering but not vengeful or wrathful.

Striking to me was the way the Redemptorists and lay missionaries and sisters listened to the people affected and saw the need for liturgical action to heal the psychically wounded. They held numerous liturgical ceremonies to bless the dead spots (where people were thought to be missing) and to grieve the dead. The other aid organizations did not know how to deal with this dimension of the crisis; even the religious persons in these agencies were not alert to the spiritual despair and grief. Clearly the priests approached the Waray people as full human beings rather than as "clients." They had had, or made, relationships with the people and took their beliefs and desires into account in working with them. This relational aspect of the priests' work is exemplary in undertaking charity and may further suggest how local churches and organizations can be more effective than international groups swooping in to help.

As we have stated, charity or relief is a short-term response to a devastating event. These are very important, life-saving actions; donating to organizations that provide disaster assistance can make a lot of difference to the victims of natural or human disasters. However, every attempt should be made to provide relief in such a way as to respect the dignity and suffering of the distressed. The priority (after the initial life-saving measures) should be on local initiatives so that people can be empowered to help themselves. After all, the organizations that respond to the disaster will not be a part of the future, at least to the extent they have been in addressing the need or disaster. Even during relief and charity efforts, with few exceptions, the focus must be on rehabilitation and reconstruction.

Discussion Questions

1. What are the immediate needs of the poor and working poor in your community? How would you know whether "relief" is called for to address these needs or not?

2. What charities do you support, individually or as a congregation? What good work do they do that attracts you to support them? How do you determine which charities to support?

3. What makes a charity ambiguous or actually harmful? After reading this chapter, do you recognize any potentially harmful elements in the relief efforts you are involved in or support?

4. What are the best and worst examples of short-term missions you have witnessed? Are STMs your church is involved in typically relief oriented? How can you ensure that future efforts by your church or organization are done in a way that doesn't hurt the people you hope to help?

5. STM trips can be enriching for the volunteers as well as for those on the receiving end of relief. How can you help ensure that the "experience" of the mission does not take precedence over (or worse, actively worsen) the needs of those being served?

6. What do you think people who are caught in destructive weather like Yolanda or Katrina or Sandy feel like right after the disaster? What would be helpful to them? How might relief of material needs be carried out in such a way as not to ignore the spiritual and relational aspects of the recipients? How can charity not cripple the recipients?

7. How might the response of aid workers change if they realized that they themselves were "broken" in some way alongside the victims of disaster? In what ways are you broken or struggling? How can this brokenness inspire you to help others?

CHAPTER 4

STRATEGY 2:
SELF-HELP

The second strategy we discuss is self-help, also called self-development or self-determination. In both of the first two strategies, relief and self-help, the people developing their abilities benefit from the assistance of others. However, self-help is preferable when the situation, even though it may be dire, does not have the same immediacy or short duration that appropriately calls for relief. It also depends on the recipients being willing to work with another person or agency toward their own self-development or self-sufficiency. Broadly speaking, they will be building their skill capacity to acquire a better quality of life. They might be described as receiving support, but the primary emphasis is on their own participation.

As we noted in the last chapter, even the way relief is administered to people in desperate circumstances involves an awareness that charity is not the norm. It is not the normal position that self-sufficiency is, and relief should be conducted in a way that builds into self-help. Some elements of this strategy overlap with cultural formation and also governmental policy—our third and fourth strategies.

One must have both capacities and opportunities to achieve a decent standard of living. So a person or family needs to develop the abilities or skills to do a particular job and have a chance to earn a livelihood. There must also be an opportunity to put those capacities to work. All of us who work can point to the structures that enabled us to develop capacities and also to opportunities to use those capacities. Most of the time there were people who helped us develop, and also there were jobs to be had. If one does not have capacities or any means of developing them, and if there are no opportunities to earn a living, then one winds up living in poverty or with a job that perpetuates one's asset-limited status. Inequalities develop in these ways.

When U.S. citizens are asked about whether inequality is a high priority, they respond in telling ways. On the one hand, in response to a January 2015 CBS/*New York Times* poll asking what the top national issue was, only 3 percent cited the income gap between rich and poor. At the same time, however, 18 percent saw "the economy and jobs" as the top issue.[1] A Reason-Rupe poll in August 2014 on whether Congress should focus on increasing economic growth or reducing income inequality found that 74 percent of the people voted for growth, only 20 percent for reducing inequality. At the same time, other surveys found that 78 percent thought income inequality was a "big problem" and 66 percent thought that Congress should do something about it.[2] These results may seem contradictory or at least inconsistent at first glance, but the message is quite clear. When people feel that their own income may be negatively affected by distribution, they are far more inclined to vote for growth; they fear that voting for reducing inequality might mean cutting their benefits through redistribution. This may be especially true for seniors who depend on Social Security.[3] However, it should be noted that, personal incomes aside, a growing number of people believe that it is vital to increase the income of those on the bottom rung of the ladder and support the middle class. If those are identified as working people, the numbers for fostering economic growth for all would almost certainly rise.

Central to the American dream is the notion that hard work will pay off. However, some companies are engaging in practices that keep the incomes of the working poor at a low level. E. J. Dionne, writing in the *Washington Post* on July 1, 2015, uncovers some of these practices. Some businesses, he writes, are "setting up workers as franchisees or owners of limited liability companies" to "shield" themselves "from tax and labor statutes."[4] This is a case of shifting risk off corporate balance sheets and onto the shoulders of individual Americans. In contrast, as we shall see, other companies are exemplary in promoting the self-development of their employees—for example, by helping to finance employees' educational expenses and working with them to increase their skills and usefulness to the company.

What Constitutes Self-Help?

The distinction between relief and self-help can be illustrated through a couple of examples.

One project that helps lower-income people achieve better jobs is Project Light in Manatee County, Florida. Adults from the Caribbean, Latin America, and Eastern Europe learn English, math, and computer skills in classes at the literacy center in Bradenton. "We're very proud at what we've been able to achieve," says Luz Corcuera, Project Light board member and director of the Healthy Start Coalition of Manatee County. "Students from all backgrounds have come here and eventually moved onto college or different careers. It's all about getting a better job instead of having to work two or three at a time."[5]

Consider this program from Oklahoma which enables children to help themselves in the long run. There, four-year-olds—even those from underprivileged homes—have access to a year of high-quality pre-kindergarten. There are also programs to coach parents on reading and talking more to their kids. The program intends to break the cycle of poverty through education.

Nick Kristof wrote about two girls, ages three and four, whom he met in one Tulsa school. Their great-grandmother had her first child at thirteen. Their grandmother had her first at fifteen. The mom had her first by thirteen, born with drugs in his system, and she now has four children by three fathers.

"But these two girls," he writes, "thriving in a pre-school may break that cycle. Their step-great-grandmother, Patricia Ann Gaines, is raising them and getting coaching from the school on how to read to them frequently, and she is determined to see them reach the middle class.

"I want them to go to college, be trouble-free, have no problem with incarceration," she said.

Students who take advantage of the pre-school program wind up a half-year ahead of where they would be without it. "We've seen a huge change in terms of not only academically the preparation they have been taking into kindergarten, but also socially," said Kirt Hartzler, the superintendent of Union Public Schools in Tulsa. "It's a huge jump-start for kids."[6]

This program is partly due to the influence of George B. Kaiser, a Tulsa billionaire who sought to find a program that would have the highest social return for his charitable investment. It addresses a structure that can have lifelong results. It might also be noted that the results of the program are not automatic but depend on children and relatives being willing and able to make the emotional and time investment in helping themselves.

Mixing Relief and Self-Help

While these initiatives contain elements of charity—wealthy donors, free services—the difference is important: people who help themselves or avail themselves of assistance offered by others have contributed to their own development. Catholic ethicist Monika Hellwig suggests that being able to make such a contribution is one of our essential needs as human beings; it is important for us to have something to give, and in these self-help programs, that something is effort.[7] Furthermore, the vital component of self-help enables participants to feel empowered and in fact to be empowered. The skill and knowledge they gain cannot be taken away; through them they can access jobs, find a voice, and have a sense of participating in the wider society.

There is, I am suggesting, a continuum of the mixture of subsidy or relief elements and self-help contributions by recipients. In this chapter our examples of self-help begin with those that have a large component of relief and proceed toward those that are more purely self-help. One continuously controversial program that mixes relief and self-help is the Supplemental Nutrition Assistance Program (SNAP), or food stamps. Consider for a moment the difference between the sort of help that Peace Presbyterian provided immediately for two weeks to a destitute family (discussed in chapter 3 as an example of relief) and the sort of long-term continuity that food stamps and housing programs can offer. These latter provide a floor that can enable ALICE and ALEC to move into self-sufficiency.

Greg Kaufmann, poverty correspondent for the *Nation*, speaking to Bill Moyers in 2013, says, "People are working and they're not getting paid enough to feed their families, pay their utilities and pay for their housing, pay for the healthcare. . . . If you're not paying people enough to pay for the basics, they're going to need help getting food."[8] Kaufmann points out that millions of working adults struggling to make ends meet, children, disabled people, and the elderly are assisted by food stamps.

The evidence suggests that SNAP has been effective in reducing the number of food-insecure households so that recipients could work. It has reached those most in need in the United States and reduced the special health-care needs of children, alleviated maternal depression, and reduced suicidal impulses and poor sleep habits.[9] A study at the University of California–Davis by Dr. Hilary Hoynes and others in 2012 looked at the outcomes for adults who had had access to food stamps as children or even before their birth. It found that "the adults had significant reductions in metabolic illnesses such as heart disease, diabetes, obesity, high blood pressure. And even more remarkable . . . was women in particular had higher earnings, higher income, higher educational attainment and less reliance on welfare assistance in general." For these reasons, it seems that SNAP is as much a program promoting self-help as it is relief. In fact, Kaufmann draws this conclusion when he says that "all these years" its opponents "have been saying it's promoting dependence, and it's been building self-reliance."[10]

SNAP may be even more significant, given the recent report that "a staggering price hike in housing costs" makes it difficult for low-income Americans "to afford basic necessities." The Pew Charitable Trusts analyzed data from the Bureau of Labor Statistics that indicated that rising prices impacted those with low income disproportionately and were also affecting middle-income families.[11] At least those with SNAP benefits can come closer to paying the rent and helping themselves.

The numbers are telling. The U.S. Agriculture Department's Web site on SNAP indicates households whose gross monthly income is at 130 percent of the poverty level are eligible, on average, for food stamps.[12] A family of four making less than $24,300 net income a year could receive up to $649 a month.

In 2011, "28 percent of workers . . . made wages that were less than the poverty line. Poverty wages," Kaufmann says. "Fifty percent of the jobs in this country make less than $34,000 a year. Twenty-five percent make less than the poverty line for a family of four."[13]

By helping people meet their basic needs, food stamps are encouraging self-help. Without the assistance of SNAP, there would be considerably more ALECs in this country. By definition these are people who are working hard to get by, and to the extent that they can, that is due in part to food stamps. Furthermore, able-bodied recipients of food stamps are required to seek out employment counseling and to work or volunteer for eighty hours a month. Thus they are encouraged toward self-help.

Housing as Vital to Self-Help

Further along the continuum are programs which recognize that many working people experience a catastrophic event that, if the ensuing situation persists or worsens, could result in homelessness. The Center for Public Ministry in Dubuque, Iowa (with which I was privileged to work), provided two apartment houses for working people who were earning enough to disqualify them for other sorts of assistance but not so much that they were able to afford an apartment or home. We charged rock-bottom rates, the objective being that people who were able to work but needed some stable housing could manage, in a reasonable amount of time, to move out of this decent, but not attractive, alternative. Our goal was to provide a way station on the path out of low-income jobs. A manager who lived on-site assisted the residents in that process.

A similar effort is under way in Tampa, Florida. Lionni and Cherisa Bayard were sleeping in their car after being evicted from their apartment. After finding housing in the new homeless shelter of the Drug Abuse Comprehensive Coordinating Office, they were able to get back on their feet in only three weeks. More a dormitory than a home, this facility provides shelter, clothes, and food, and allows residents to regroup and restart. It enables working people to ride out a storm and have a stable base while they are seeking work or looking for a better job.[14]

Habitat for Humanity is perhaps the best-known self-help program. It offers financial assistance for a family who work alongside local volunteers to build the house that they will live in. They can buy that house on comfortable terms over a long time. The phrase that has become synonymous with Habitat is "sweat equity," recognizing that those who have a stake in their own development and achievement of a stable living situation are more committed to it. Some of the decisions about the new home are made by those who will live there and own the house.

Self-Help through Education

A number of businesses, social service agencies, and other groups have seen the value of subsidizing their employees' or clients' college education or offering education benefits for their children. A prominent recent example is Starbucks, which is offering tuition reimbursement for all its baristas who work more than twenty hours a week. Three-quarters of Starbucks employees, and the same proportion of American adults, do not have a bachelor's degree. In her extensive article in the *Atlantic* about the program, "How to Graduate from Starbucks," Ripley reports that many of the baristas had dropped out of college as a result of loan repayment requirements and the bureaucratic logistics that college students must negotiate to receive financial aid.[15] For example, the Free Application for Federal Student Aid (FAFSA) is a maze of questions that requires access to last year's tax returns and an estimate of this year's. This form is required for a Pell Grant that could assist lower-income students. Furthermore, the earlier in the year one fills it out, the more likely it is that one will actually get assistance. For students who may be the first in their families to even apply to college, the process can be especially daunting. There is almost a sign over the application door: "No one in the lower 40 income percentile need apply."

It is to the credit of Starbucks CEO Howard Schultz and Arizona State University President Michael Crow that the two institutions teamed up to help Starbucks employees take ASU courses online and finish their degrees. Make no mistake; the student must work hard, often holding down two jobs, to graduate from college and move on to a better-paying job. This is only a subsidy, not charity, and there are still obstacles for lower-income students. "We have set up incredibly complex universities with rules that most of the faculty have trouble figuring out," says Arizona State University vice provost Timothy M. Renick. "Then we hand students a course catalog and say 'Find your way.'" Between 1970 and 2012, the proportion of twenty-four-year-olds with a bachelor's degree rose from 40 percent to 73 percent among those from affluent families, but only from 6 percent to 8 percent among those from low-income families. The fact that many children of low-income and working-class parents do not finish college explains more about the income gap in the United States than do "declining union membership, frayed social services, [and] low minimum wages," says Anthony P. Carnevale, the director of Georgetown University Center on Education and the Workforce.[16]

The relative success of the Starbucks–Arizona State initiative is due to many factors, and we will look at this as an example of the strategy of action by public institutions in the next chapter. Two things about the implementation of the self-help strategy were key to helping baristas achieve a bachelor's degree. One is the use of coaches throughout the process. Others call such coaches "mentors" who help the student negotiate the FAFSA forms, teach time-management skills, and handle bureaucratic snafus that many middle-class parents and students already know how to handle. Mentors step in with those skills that are simply presumed among middle-class and upper-class students. Calling it "the most revolutionary part of the program," Ripley cites the way all enrolled employees are given individualized guidance—a benefit that many elite universities give their students. Each student has an enrollment counselor, a financial-aid adviser, an academic adviser, and a "success coach." Arizona State, 40 percent of whose students come from low-income families, already had in place eAdvisor, which provides guidance as to which classes to take and tracks student progress. In addition, the program employs enrollment counselors. Also, there is a weeklong orientation for online learners from Starbucks and the ongoing support of a success coach. Even with all that support, the program generated a disappointingly small number of students at first. This is where the second key comes in.

When the program was not achieving the expected level of success, rather than the initiators' trying to figure out the reasons themselves or simply concluding the effort, the program asked the Starbucks student-employees what was impeding it. Starbucks and ASU then modified the program. "The concept of listening to students—and then making structural changes based on their feedback—remains unheard-of at most colleges," asserts Ripley.[17] In the next chapter, we will look at the success of this strategy from the corporate side of the ledger.

Low-income people have long used education to become financially mobile. It is heartening to discover programs that enable schoolchildren to achieve their potential. In the wake of the 9/11 terrorist attack, a child psychiatrist was assigned to uncover the sorts of trauma that event had on schoolchildren. Pamela Cantor found that the children's trauma was due less to that violent event than to the everyday chaos and lack of safety in the schools. In effect, the school system was having the same influence as the disordered and unsafe community the students lived in. Cantor called it a "hugely negative culture" that was producing high stress levels and blocking learning. "Low-performing schools tend to share high stress, negative cultures (lots of yelling, punishments and inconsistent responses from adults), students . . . who are two to four years behind grade level," and teachers and administrators who have not been trained to take on these challenges.[18]

Enter Turnaround for Children. This organization combats the effects of these schools' culture by designing an environment that will "set development on a healthy course."[19] Turnaround enlists the whole school, inviting everyone in the school community to participate. The principal must have a vision of a different culture; teachers must learn how to encourage learning and build trust; students must take responsibility for their education; and parents must support this effort. Ninety percent of the students with behavioral needs get connected to appropriate services, usually within three weeks. This is in contrast to the average of only 20 percent of students getting needed mental-health services. Cantor argues that the program succeeds because it focuses on nonacademic skills as a foundation for the development of academic ones. "Children's cognitive, social and emotional development is wired," she says. "If we set up an environment to be rich in relationships it will allow that development to flourish—and with that the expression of the full potential in every child."[20]

The next case builds on the insights of Turnaround but goes even further.

Perhaps the most astounding example of self-help through education comes from Jennings, Missouri, which borders Ferguson, where the Black Lives Matter movement gained national attention through street demonstrations after the death of Michael Brown in 2014. The superintendent of the Jennings School District, which serves about three thousand students in a low-income, predominantly African American jurisdiction just north of St. Louis, was "determined to clear the barriers that so often keep poor children from learning."[21] Now the Jennings School District operates a homeless shelter and food bank and provides clothing for its students. It makes pediatricians and mental health counselors available to students, and even provides washers and dryers so that students can go to school with clean clothes. Seventeen-year-old Gwen McDile was one student who benefitted. Homeless in the fall of 2015, she had missed so much school—nearly one day in three—that it seemed doubtful she would graduate in June. Just after Thanksgiving, however, she moved into Hope House, the shelter the district had recently opened for homeless students. With food in the pantry and a safe place to live, her attendance and study habits improved. By mid-December, she had gotten a job, was performing in a school show, and was confident she would graduate on time. Her remarkable reversal and the other stories of hope that are coming out of the Jennings district are evidence that with help, students whose backgrounds are dismal can make it.

Social Programs That Work

There are social programs that produce healthy benefits; the programs that have been evaluated and found to help people do better in life deserve our attention. "A growing body of evidence shows that a few model social programs—home visits to vulnerable families, K–12 education, pregnancy prevention, community college and employment training—produce solid impacts that can last for many years," writes Ron Haskins, codirector of the Center on Children and Families at the Brookings Institution.[22]

A common feature of these programs is a visiting partner or coach who comes alongside the low-income person to assist them in learning, for example, how to develop life skills. In Lancaster County, Pennsylvania, the Nurse Family Partnership serves first-time mothers by forming close relationships with them and advising them on prenatal health and child-rearing issues. Visits by these nurses continue, with decreasing frequency, until the child is two. Measured results indicate that these mothers are less abusive, that they are working more than unvisited low-income moms, and that their children are more likely to be ready for school.

Many of these programs are voluntary and involve steady contact and friendly partnership such as exists in many Big Brothers and Big Sisters programs. Notice how many similarities these programs share with the Seattle–King County Healthy Homes Projects described later in this chapter. While it is difficult to know with certainty why these programs have positive results, it is clear that evaluating their success and proceeding with those that have created evidence-based improvements is money and effort well invested.

Churches initiate similar programs. Besides offering food pantries, churches also help people learn how to cook, teach good nutrition, conduct financial education, and accompany working and low-income people as grocery shoppers and friends. A Hispanic ministry in Bradenton, the Beth-El Minstries, is staffed by church volunteers who sort, fill, and distribute food bags. They also initiated a tutoring and youth ministry program that adds the component of getting to know kids and working alongside them. Many churches which begin doing work that is largely relief move into more group-oriented ministries. Churches often provide health services and also community development work.

The Importance of Self-Determination

One characteristic of successful self-help groups stands out over and over again, so much so that it must be noted. To improve neighborhoods, the people who live there must have a hand in deciding their fate. It is this matter of investing oneself and contributing to the decision making that characterizes successful programs.

The approach of local decision making has worked well in Houston, Texas. There, a nonprofit organization called Neighborhood Centers grew up out of the settlement house movement. Angela Blanchard, the organization's president and chief executive officer, said the neighborhood's people were not the problem but rather "the asset, the source of potential solutions." By "spending hundreds of hours conducting one-on-one interviews and community meetings, inviting residents to specify their priorities," this organization has succeeded in determining what the neighborhood members want. They have secured funds from thirty-seven state, federal, and local programs and have seventy sites across the city.[23]

Sometimes the best people to provide information and care in a self-development project are those from the neighborhood who understand the situation because they are there themselves. This was the case in the Seattle–King County Healthy Homes Project, which had as its goal the improvement of the asthma-related health status of low-income children by reducing exposure to allergens and irritants in their homes. (Asthma is the most common chronic disease of children, especially among low-income children and children of color.) Under the auspices of Seattle Partners for Healthy Communities,

Resources for Promoting Self-Help

There are countless ways to offer assistance to those who want to improve their life situation through improving their skills, locating jobs (or better jobs), and achieving the stability necessary to thrive. Search for volunteer opportunities with the **United Way**'s network of programs. https://www.unitedway.org/get -involved/volunteer/

Partnering with a local school is a great way to invest in your community, by tutoring students who need extra help, providing school supplies, or organizing fund-raisers, clothing drives, and food drives to make sure children have what they need to succeed. To identify schools in your area that might be most in need of help, visit **School Digger** and search your area by performance ratings or percentage of children receiving free and reduced-price lunches. www.schooldigger.com

There are also established programs that bring adults alongside children and adults who are developing their capacities in public education, in household finance, and in becoming eligible for jobs. **Reading Partners** mobilizes volunteers to work with individual students so that they can read at grade level by fourth grade. www.readingpartners.org

Habitat for Humanity builds homes for—and with—people in need of housing stability. There are ways to get involved even if manual labor isn't an option for you, such as making meals for those doing construction, teaching financial literacy, and mentoring new homeowners. www.habitat.org

Heifer International operates globally and domestically to send animals to promote self-development among people without resources. Children especially get excited about giving gifts of animals, making it a good option for annual initiatives in congregations, such as raising money to give chicks or rabbits at Easter or doing a "fill the ark" fund-raiser. www.heifer.org

community health workers (CHWs) were recruited from the communities being served by the project. All six lived within the targeted area and were either personally affected or had a family member affected by asthma. They had an "insider perspective"—an understanding of the culture and the workings of the community. They were perceived to have a more empathic understanding and to be credible sources of information and advice. Thus they provided a culturally appropriate link between the community and the medical system. In addition, they were encouraged to work holistically with the asthma-impacted families to address preventive measures.

"Rather than conducting the assessments and carrying out the change strategies *for* the families, the CHWs provided the knowledge, resources, and support necessary to empower the families to take action for themselves," write Catherine Heaney and Barbara Israel. The participants were pleased with the performance of their CHWs; 84 percent rated their CHW as excellent or very good. The effectiveness of the project was measured by comparing the results of "high-intensity" and "low-intensity" involvement of the CHW with the family. Children in the high-intensity group had fewer days of activity affected by asthma and fewer times when urgent health services were used. Children's caregivers in the high-intensity group reported more improvement in quality of life as well. The authors found that these gains were sustained for at least six months.[24]

When Candace Keshwar emigrated from Trinidad to Boston in 2002, she had a dream of getting a college education and career, but that was jeopardized when her first daughter was born with cerebral palsy. For the next seven years she looked after her daughter while her husband worked construction and the family depended on government assistance. "It was a real dark space for me," she says. But Candace joined a group from low-income communities who have organized themselves in order to achieve their goals. Called the Family Independence Initiative, it creates structures for families that encourage a sense of control. By pooling resources, such as day care and transportation, it encourages self-help and aids mothers and fathers achieve their goals. Candace and others are finishing college and beginning careers through this strategy.[25]

ALICE and ALEC organizing themselves to create networks of support multiplies their impact. Another example is a group of first-generation, low-income college students who sit in classes learning about the sociology of poverty, which they themselves have experienced, and who tire of seeking to pass as middle class. Ana Barros decided to "come out" and join as well as lead the Harvard College First Generation Student Union, whose purpose is to offer students in the same situation a place to share the realities of being first-generation students. These are empowering and information-sharing support systems. Many of the members come from minority groups and families whose income is radically different from the average at the mostly white elite colleges.[26] In these examples we see the operation of groups working to understand their cultures of origin that impede self-help and those innovative cultural initiatives which seek to change that culture.

The strategy of self-help exemplified there begins to move into our third strategy: influencing cultural values and movements that empower working-class people and promote the flourishing of all.

Discussion Questions

1. What is the major difference between the strategies of relief and self-help? How are they related? Can you name a program that emphasizes self-development in your community?

2. Name two or three people or groups that have enabled you to develop your abilities. Does ALICE have access to similar sources of help and guidance? What skills do you and others in your church have in which you could mentor others?

3. Food stamps (or SNAP) can be a hot-button issue. How do you feel about food stamps for those at 130 percent of the poverty level? How do relief-type programs like food stamps or free housing contribute to self-sufficiency?

4. Are there relief programs your church is involved in that could be expanded to promote self-help? Think about the factors that lead people to need relief aid repeatedly; what sorts of self-help could break that cycle of dependency?

5. Do you think free college education is a workable strategy to enable ALICE and ALEC to improve their economic situation? Does it make economic sense for companies like Starbucks to subsidize their employees' education?

6. How can parents and schools work together to improve children's education rather than conflict with each other?

7. The upshot of the chapter is that self-determination is essential for helping people reach their potential. Does the idea of helping someone help themselves feel oxymoronic to you? How do we help while letting people maintain control over their own trajectory?

8. One of the last examples in this chapter includes a self-organized group of ALECs. How can we offer support for and express solidarity with ALICEs who are beginning to organize?

CHAPTER 5

STRATEGY 3:
CULTURAL FORMATION

This third strategy can be difficult to describe, as it is not identi-fied with only one group or one type of action. Developing a cul-ture that promotes the flourishing of all people includes policies and initiatives by businesses, voluntary associations, or actions on behalf of certain classes of people—women, LGBT persons, low-wage workers or tenants—fighting for their rights. What links all of these is the fact that they influence cultural values or public opinion. We are all part of such organizations, whether they are political parties, churches, neighborhood groups, informal small-scale associations, media outlets, corporations, citizen organizations, or civic groups. They include unions, denominational agencies, charitable foundations, and broader social movements. This strategy goes beyond self-help groups because the groups considered in this chapter are organized to influence opinion; they do not have the formal power of courts of law or of state and federal government. This is the realm of cultural influence, or value formation.

These efforts are not about providing direct assistance to those in distress (relief), nor do they depend on the participation of those being supported (self-help), but their influence pervades all the other strategies. We might see this as almost a type of politics, swaying public opinion and possibly resulting in laws and policies (though the content of those laws and policies is the realm of the strategy of government action, the focus of the next chapter). The 2016 political campaigns of Donald Trump and Bernie Sanders are good examples of social or cultural movements that fed off of people's discontent with the government and galvanized, even legitimated, the anger of many working people and also younger people facing an uncertain future. The strategy of cultural formation depends on persuasion and influence more than on direct action. It happens at a community level, where values are shaped and people are socialized.

Our social attitudes have become far more consequential as the issues we face have become more global. Globalization — whether through the economy, the climate, or immigration — affects us every day. Racial and ethnic conflicts in the United States and abroad, refugee crises, and wars among and within different nations have made us deeply aware that these issues are integrally connected. We almost take this for granted, even though how our government handles such global issues is influenced by our opinion.

One example of the intersection of cultural values and public policy is the U.S. tax code's treatment of charitable giving. The deduction for donations encourages voluntary giving to churches and other organizations, which reflects a cultural value that giving is worthwhile. Tax-deductible donations are essential to social programs that assist ALICE, and while the deduction may be seen as self-serving, the policy helps perpetuate a culture where helping others matters. Similarly, businesses often provide health insurance, life insurance, and other benefits that enable people to improve their quality of life. Such benefits have become law in many cases, and yet many companies go beyond what is required by law, reflecting a cultural value of supporting the well-being of employees. Howard Schultz, the president of Starbucks, has stated that "we're living at a time when for-profit public companies must redefine their responsibilities to the communities they serve and to their employees."[1] Schultz believes that businesses have a responsibility to their publics. He is expressing a value and trying to influence public opinion. Not only has the company he represents participated in self-help programs, it is also generating a cultural value. In this chapter, we focus on the ways in which cultural values are rebalancing the forces that have disadvantaged ALICE.

Movements for Fair Wages

To illustrate the power of cultural and social movements, consider the history of the Fight for $15 (as a minimum wage) movement. From November 2012, when a one-day fast-food workers' strike at McDonald's was labeled "laughable" or "pie in the sky," to April 2016, when a minimum wage of $15 an hour had been adopted as legislation by the states of New York and California, it has been a powerful social movement that shows the power of public opinion and values. In "How the $15 Minimum Wage Went from Laughable to Viable," Steven Greenhouse credits a number of factors: "a lot of pro-labor, pro-worker sentiment"; public opinion (59 percent of Americans polled support the $15 minimum); "frustration over wage stagnation and income inequality"; and public disenchantment with low-paying service jobs.[2] Those factors have generated a protest movement that, in our democracy, translates into a cultural force. The success of that movement owes a great deal to the pressure that public demonstrations and supporters of the goal brought to bear on legislators.

The Fair Food Program of the Coalition of Immokalee Workers is another group using public pressure to influence change. Beginning as a representative for tomato pickers, many of whom are immigrants, the coalition pressed for a penny-a-pound raise and also for legislation that would improve their working and living conditions. The extra penny per pound wouldn't come out of the growers' profits but from corporate buyers like groceries and restaurant chains. While that penny a pound does not sound like much to those in the middle class, for workers in the tomato fields, that and other changes are huge: "time clocks, outdoor shade, and eighty extra bucks a week." Consider one Immokalee worker's story:

Mely Perez is a twenty-four-year-old single mom who works the tomato fields. For her the extra cash represents not just more cash for household expenses but the ability to make her young sons breakfast in the morning and walk them to school. Before she had to sneak out of the house before the sun rose to catch a bus for the fields. She did not see them until she arrived home at night exhausted.

Furthermore, the benefits of the Fair Food program may have extended to the town's economy. Bradley Muckel, head of the Immokalee [Florida] Community Redevelopment Agency reports that this has probably spurred some commercial projects in the town of Immokalee as well.[3]

This story illustrates the necessity of perseverance and of corporate action to achieve economic goals. It is not enough for union leaders, Bradley Muckel, or Mely Perez to act alone. They were able to realize greater equality through group effort. Other actors include the Presbyterian Church (U.S.A.), which endorsed a boycott of Publix, a large grocery chain in Florida, for not joining the Fair Food Program. Kudos to Walmart, Subway, and other corporate tomato buyers who were willing to pay an extra penny a pound on to the farmworkers.

The Fair Food Program is a unique partnership among farmers, farmworkers, and retail food companies that ensures humane wages and working conditions for the workers who pick fruits and vegetables on participating farms. It harnesses the power of consumer demand to give farmworkers a voice in the decisions that affect their lives and to eliminate the long-standing abuses that have plagued agriculture. This is a fine example of ethical consumerism, by which consumers press for conditions and wages that benefit workers. Directed consumer demand by individuals and organizations, including churches, can make a difference.

The strategy of culture formation or action recognizes the need for large-scale adoption of projects that embody certain values. In order to make relief and self-help work, we need the support of networks of people who support those specific strategies. In the absence of such public opinion, the move toward enabling those strategies will probably fail. Another example of this is the widespread awareness and acceptance of microenterprise as a way of helping others. With the help of organizations such as Grameen Bank, kiva.org, and others, people are able to lend money to minority and international enterprises that can empower local businesses. The growth in popularity of such microenterprises represents the acceptance of an easy way to engage in charity.

Throughout this chapter we recommend that those who would support ALICE and ALEC join organizations that support the spread of distributive and democratic values. While it is true that there is no economic system that perfectly aligns with Christianity, there are policies and organizations that are definitely more compassionate and more even-handed than others.

Developing Social Capital

In chapters 3 and 4, we have been able to point to tangible actions and programs that were successful in assisting working-class people to improve their lives if they would participate in them. Now we come to this community-wide, if not nationwide, intangible called "culture" or "public opinion" or "social values," which can be measured or approximated from some manifestations but which is more difficult to visualize. We are talking about social networks and location. The two come together on the neighborhood level where neighbors cooperate with neighbors for mutual benefit.

Jan and Cornelia Butler Flora use the term "social capital" in their community development research.[4] By that they mean a network of social organizations that develop relationships and social trust. In shorthand, this could be labeled "community"; it represents the somewhat romantic notion of what a rural town or hamlet used to be. Images come to mind of fictional Mayberry, where the virtues of honesty and neighborliness govern everyday life.

Perhaps it would be helpful to contrast this with the description of what has happened to Robert Putnam's hometown of Port Clinton, Ohio, which indicates how the amount of social capital there has declined.[5] Putnam argues that the egalitarian world in which he grew up is gone, a victim of widening income gaps, hence the underappreciated changes in family life, neighborhoods, and schools. He indicates that when he was growing up in Port Clinton, there was a strong sense that children belonged to everyone in the community and everyone had a stake in their future. There was high social capital there. That, reports Putnam, has evaporated in the gap between the advantages enjoyed by the upwardly mobile rich and the disadvantages experienced by the downwardly mobile working class. This sort of fractionalization by income is happening nationwide and worsens ALICE's situation.

The shaping power of the community in which we grow up is gaining increased attention in the social sciences. Social capital has to do with social networks and social support; as such, the level of care that the child receives while growing up is vital. If that care is missing or there is neglect and abuse, that obviously has a powerful impact. If we are looking for a quantifiable measure to predict the social capital of a neighborhood, then we would turn to the income level of the community and the quality of the schools in that district.

In a gem of an essay hidden away in a social work text, Catherine A. Heaney and Barbara A. Israel explore the way that social relationships impact health.[6] We can think about the influence of the type of social support that is in place for those belonging to various networks. For a concrete notion of "network of support," think of a family, a gang, a town, a church choir, a parent-teacher association, or an economic cooperative. While they obviously vary in degree of involvement and intensity of support, they all generate social capital. The strength of the social network and the exchange of social support may increase or decrease a community's ability to access resources and solve problems. Furthermore, the culture in a neighborhood could be detrimental as well as positive, and the "social support" network might be one that encourages crime.

Heaney and Israel concluded that a community with strong social capital would enhance preventive health habits and lower the overall incidence of disease. They discovered that health professionals were less effective in providing social support day-to-day than were community health workers. While the professionals had knowledge and resources, it was the trained members of the community who had "empathetic understanding" and on-site presence to improve the health of the sick.[7] The use of lay indigenous natural helpers and community health workers suggests that the overall health of a community can be enhanced. This sort of learning can be used in towns and neighborhoods of working-class people who are ALICEs and ALECs. Networks can be enhanced through community capacity building and problem solving. Local networks carry the social values that are operating nationally.

The Shaping Power of Neighborhood

These research findings interface with the revived discovery that location matters—one's place of residence can intensify the harmful effects of a culture of lower-income households. The latest book to make this case is *Evicted: Poverty and Profit in the American City*, in which Matthew Desmond describes what it is like to live in a trailer park and a rooming house on the poverty-stricken North Side of Milwaukee. The exorbitant rents and horrifying conditions of this housing are scary. It is often black women who are evicted with their children.[8] Imagine the forces that are set in motion that drag children (and their parents) into dysfunctional living.

The dynamics of a place-based culture may, alternatively, intensify the benefits of living in a privileged, affluent neighborhood. Tina Rosenberg, in *Join the Club: How Peer Pressure Can Transform the World*, found that our reference groups reinforce characteristics that the group has in common (e.g., Republicans hang out with Republicans, wealthy with wealthy, fat with fat, poor with poor).[9] What could be hidden beneath her focus, however, is that these groups are segregated by location or that they self-segregate by location. Charles Murray discovered that there were pockets of affluence (which he labeled "Belmont") and pockets of disadvantage ("Fishtown") that tended to reinforce the norms of the community, whether those norms were disruptive of self-improvement or not. So, in terms of marriage, Murray discovered that people in Fishtown were divorcing and cohabiting more and simply not entering into marriage as readily as they had in the past. The decline in the marriage rate was remarkable. However, in Belmont the people were marrying just as often as they had in the past and, furthermore, the rate of divorce had remained steady over several decades.[10] My point here is that when the media discusses "the end of marriage," what lurks behind those statistics is that one group in working-class locations is divorcing, cohabiting, or never marrying far more than another. In short, averages can disguise and generalize the particular.

The influence of housing itself is hard to overestimate. The need for stability in one's life goes beyond the physical necessity for shelter; being able to count on continuity in the place where one lives is a cultural value as well. A recent NPR blog revealed the health benefits of decent housing. Fazia Ayesh used to live in a cramped one-bedroom apartment with her family of five. It was in terrible shape, with chipping paint, no heat, drafty windows; the final straw came when Fazia's daughters got full-blown cases of asthma. The doctor told her that this was probably due to lead poisoning. In a poll, 40 percent of lower-income Americans like Ayesh, with household incomes under $25,000 a year, told NPR "they believe that poor neighborhoods and housing conditions lead to poor health."

Interviewed by Patti Neighmond, Ayesh told the story of how she applied for and qualified for subsidized housing built by

Bridge Housing. Bridge Housing is transforming communities in California and the Pacific Northwest by making sure residents have quality homes, vibrant neighborhoods, and opportunities to thrive. Working with community partners, Bridge seeks to impact education and social and health outcomes for children and families in neighborhoods. The organization seeks to mobilize community services across the spectrum of need; it is active as Rebuild Potrero in San Francisco and as Jordan Downs in Watts. This sort of holistic effort is seeking to research best practices, apply lessons learned, and practice scale in its integrated housing and community development efforts across its existing and future portfolio.[11] Bridge Housing ventures build hope and stability as well as decent housing.

Affordable housing also is a challenge in the area of Sarasota and Manatee Counties, Florida, where one in five families spend half of their income for housing.[12]

If you're poor and live in the Sarasota area, it's better to be in Charlotte County than in Manatee or Sarasota. In comparisons of future earnings, Manatee County is below average "in helping poor children up the income ladder." It ranks 1,968th out of 2,478 counties nationwide, better than only about 21 percent of counties.[13] A study by Harvard economists Raj Chetty and Nathaniel Hendren, when read in combination with an important study they wrote with Lawrence Katz, makes the most compelling case yet that good neighbors nurture success. The studies are comprehensive for all of the counties in the United States.

In the middle to late 1990s, the federal government studied the impact of an experiment, Moving to Opportunity, in which 4,600 low-income families entered a lottery that enabled them to move to better neighborhoods. The results of that change initially proved quite disappointing. The move appeared to make no appreciable difference in the employment and earnings of parents. There were some positive effects for children.

In 2015 Chetty, Hendren, and Katz restudied the effects on the same families. They found that the number of years living in a better neighborhood made quite a difference. Children who had moved as toddlers had enjoyed the benefit of years of living in that neighborhood. The results of the previous study—which combined the effects on all ages of children— hid two distinct findings: first, children who moved when they were young enjoyed much greater economic success in later years than children who had not won the lottery that enabled them to move; and second, children who moved when they were older experienced no gains and perhaps worse outcomes. If the preteens moved to a more income-integrated neighborhood, they went on to earn 31 percent more in their midtwenties than those who did not win the chance to move. They were also more likely to attend college.[14]

Significantly the grandchildren of those who had moved to a better neighborhood—the children of the children who grew up in communities with more social capital—experienced lasting positive effects. The girls grew up to live in better neighborhoods as adults, enjoyed higher incomes, and tended to raise children in two-parent homes. In short, the effects of growing up in "better" locations persisted over several generations. One test of their conclusions was the displacement of communities that happened in New Orleans because of Hurricane Katrina. When whole neighborhoods are displaced, if those communities move to better areas, their children's futures tend to improve. The restudy provides the most comprehensive and well-researched recent study of the synergistic dynamics of social capital and upward mobility in a geographic location. Simply stated, the fact is that place matters—fixing neighborhoods that drag children down or keep them in low-income conditions pays off for ALICE.

This study also suggests that, if working-class people are attempting to maintain or improve their income and life situation, they would do well to live in the best neighborhood they can afford. It is also worth recognizing that middle-class African American families tend to live in neighborhoods where their income puts them at a comparative advantage in regard to other African Americans, but below the quality of housing that white Americans with the same income could afford. In short, they either choose against or are restricted by segregation from living in neighborhoods that reflect their incomes accurately. Given the study by Chetty, Hendren, and Katz, that puts their children at a disadvantage proportionate to their income.

Adding support to the theory of the benefit of developing social capital (or the liability of dissolving it) is what Tina Rosenberg describes in *Join the Club*. We note what might happen, however, if a neighborhood group decided to reclaim their neighborhood. As they began to work, there would be a social momentum that ideally would begin to reverse the norm of letting properties or relationships erode. The value of taking pride in the neighborhood might well result in a higher quality of life for ALEC. The differences might be gradual and intangible, but the changing ethos of the location would be real. The point here is that working-class people can form groups that can generate social capital.

Businesses Influence Culture

One especially powerful source of cultural values is business. Businesses can impact culture for better and for worse. We noted the impact of advertising in generating discontent and consumerism in chapter 2 and the positive example of Starbucks's education initiative in chapter 4. Here we want to note the generation of positive values.

A fascinating development is the process of churches helping to establish businesses that improve communities. For example, Scott Planting and the cooperative parish in Maine he helped lead, The Mission at the Eastward, found that the most pressing need for people in his region was good jobs. He sought to find partners who would locate in the region and provide jobs, and the ministry eventually founded cooperative businesses for local residents. Another venture was that of Elaine Heath and Larry Duggins in Dallas, Texas, who initiated microchurch movements that updated the intentional community model, one of whose progenitors was monastic orders. They began by forming worshiping communities with refugees in sites plagued by poverty and social dislocation, and some of those communities began businesses to grow jobs. Ahadi Textiles Collective, for example, is a small business run by East African refugees.[15]

A new business model takes on the responsibility of assisting working-class people to achieve a better life. We have already mentioned Howard Schultz of Starbucks. Schultz and nearly forty-five big American corporations have teamed up to offer 100,000 jobs for unemployed people ages sixteen to twenty-four in 2015. The so-called 100,000 Opportunities Initiative works with some of the 5.5 million Americans who are neither studying nor working and offers full-time positions as well as apprenticeships and internships.[16] Unemployment of people in this age group is far higher than the average, and without a leg up in terms of college or work experience it portends economic instability for them now and in a few years. The other companies participating include Alaska Airlines, CVS Health, Hilton Hotels, Microsoft, Taco Bell, Target, and Walmart. In regard to cultural values, this sort of initiative gives evidence that business has wider responsibilities than to its stockholders.

A number of retailers are reforming their policies toward progressive wages, advance notice of assigned shifts, better training, and other incentives for employees. The city of San Francisco enacted a law in November 2014 that requires the largest retail stores to treat their workers more decently. Employers must give employees two weeks' notice of work schedules; if the notice is less than a week they must compensate an employee with four hours' wages. Employers must offer extra hours to current part-timers first and must treat part-timers equally with full-timers. The law applies to 12 percent of retailers in San Francisco, who employ almost half of the retail workers in the city.[17]

There are costs involved when retailers treat their employees poorly: higher absenteeism, tardiness, lower morale, shoddy service, and high turnover. It costs between $3,300 and $6,000 to train a replacement. In addition, poorly trained employees have lower productivity and make more errors. In contrast, there are clear benefits for businesses that treat their employees well. Dr. Zeynep Ton, of MIT's Sloan School of Management, along with Ananth Raman of the Harvard Business School, conducted a study for Borders, the bookstore chain. "We found that there was a huge variation in operational performance among stores that used the same information technology and offered the same incentives to employees. The performance of the best store was a whopping 43 times better than that of the worst."[18] The Gap is using this data in its job strategy. A book by Ton, *The Good Jobs Strategy*, gives examples of other highly successful retail chains that invest in their employees and operational practices: QuikTrip convenience stores, Trader Joe's supermarkets, Costco wholesale clubs, and others. Work at those outlets is more efficient and more fulfilling; costs are lower, sales and profits escalate, and customer satisfaction improves. Employees have better benefits. Corporations that operate with efficiency and with more just policies will do better than those that are inefficient. They will also help lift ALICE into the middle class.

The prevailing wisdom has been that paying higher minimum wages would result in lower employment because employers would not be able to afford to pay as many workers. A study by David Card and Alan Krueger and others tested this assumption. They looked at what happened in the fast-food sector when New Jersey raised its minimum wage and Pennsylvania did not. The Card-Krueger study found that raising the minimum wage had a positive effect on employment. Hypothesizing about the study's data, Paul Krugman suggests that the labor market is different from the commodity market. "There are important benefits, even to the employer, from paying them [workers] more: better morale, lower turnover, increased productivity. These benefits largely offset the direct effect of higher labor costs."[19]

One of the most-publicized corporate efforts is that of Dan Price of Gravity Payments, who, moved by his employees' situations as ALEC and ALICE, is phasing in a minimum salary of $70,000 and reducing his own salary from $1.1 million to $70,000. Previously he had kept wages down to protect the company, which had been battered by a recession. "I was so scarred by the recession," he said, "that I was proactively and proudly hurting my staff"[20] Reaction to the new salaries was swift. Price was vilified by some but praised by many (see the hashtag #imwithdan). He gave a name and a face to the debate about whether good wages produce growth in a business. The business magazine *Inc.* labeled him "a modern Robin Hood helping the working class by stealing from himself—and perhaps from shareholders of other companies whose bosses are now also putting employees ahead of profits. . . . Was it coincidence that Walmart, that paragon of parsimony, coughed up raises for its lowest-paid workers?" Profits have continued to grow during the years of the experiment. "I want the scorecard we have as business leaders to be not about money, but about purpose, impact, and service," Price told *Inc.* "I want those to be the things we judge ourselves on."[21] It may not be coincidental that Price has a Christian background.

Many other corporate efforts are under way. The town of Doxer-Foxcroft, in a depressed area of Maine, transformed an old wool mill into a retail-restaurant-hotel-farmers market site. This was a project of the Local Initiatives Support Corporation, which pulls together nongovernmental organizations and helps in assembling capital, providing expertise, securing construction loans, and generating community support along with creative thinking.[22]

Business leaders who understand that addressing ALEC's situation is good for business are growing in number. "There is a compelling new sense that generally very wealthy and senior business leaders are starting to understand this [income inequality] is a significant problem," says Harvard Business School professor Michael E. Porter, who wrote a study of the issue with colleagues Karen Mills and Jan Rivkin. The *New*

York *Times* reports, "Most interestingly, many executives say they believe the growing gap in income and opportunity is not just bad for the country, it is bad for business, too. It curbs consumer spending, undercuts worker morale and produces political polarization. 'Even with their business hat on, the system isn't working for them,' Professor Rivkin said."[23]

Porter and colleagues have good examples of corporations that are doing well while also assisting the working poor toward a better life. "Exxon Mobil put $125 million toward training teachers in science, technology and engineering—so that it might have skilled workers to hire later on. IBM joined with New York City to create an innovative, technology-oriented high school in Brooklyn. Southwire, a family-owned maker of wires and cables in Carrollton, Ga., tackled a shortage of high school graduates for hire by staffing a new factory entirely with students at risk of dropping out, and requiring them to stay in school to keep their jobs."[24]

Taking Action for Cultural Formation

The strategy of cultural action can seem distant from us. Influential reports and recommendations that commend remedial values can obscure the everyday ways that we contribute to social values. A softer but ultimately more influential course of action may be the persuasive power of what we buy week in and week out. Raising consciousness of inequality through the Immokalee Workers' campaigns against Publix supermarkets or Wendy's for refusing to contribute to the Fair Food Alliance is one way of bringing pressure to bear on organizations that refuse to pay more adequate wages. Or consider the impact of selling fair-trade coffee at innumerable churches week after week. Or the power of investing in microenterprises both domestically and internationally. Publicizing and patronizing those businesses and organizations that practice charity toward ALICE and ALEC and offer

Resources for Effecting Cultural Change

Cultural formation happens when we practice our values in the public sphere—our purchases, our participation in events and voluntary associations, and even our conversations and reading habits can influence others to value equality and pay attention to those who are struggling economically.

Churches can help create a culture that promotes income equality by paying fairly for the goods and services they use and encouraging congregants to do the same. **Fair Trade USA** offers information and links for finding fairly traded goods, from coffee and chocolate to clothing and home goods. http://fairtradeusa .org/products-partners

Visit the **Fair Food Program's** Web site for a regularly updated list of retailers and restaurants. www.fairfoodprogram .org/partners/

It is difficult to find a list of companies paying their employees a living wage, especially since that amount varies by location, but some companies are choosing to pay well over the minimum wage. A few companies with notable wages that may be found in your community include **Costco, Trader Joe's, Whole Foods,** and **Ben & Jerry's.**[25]

Form groups in your community to study, discuss, and take action on particular issues related to income inequality. **Moms Against Poverty** is one such group, based in California. www .momsagainstpoverty.org

living wages and adequate health insurance for their workers can influence public opinion and bolster a greater degree of income equality. So can supporting social justice organizations that work against income inequality, investigate the impact of tax codes, or seek to reform criminal justice systems that unjustly penalize those who commit property or drug crimes and destroy family systems. Volunteering at public schools to ensure that adequate attention can be paid to students in overcrowded classrooms and voting for increased subsidies for classrooms and teachers are other actions that are within our capacities.

Encouraging others in churches to investigate income inequality through sermons or adult forums (for example, by studying this book!) are other ways of exploring how to address the issues that ALICE faces. Churches and other organizations could do research into their own communities or find research that has already been done. Joining their efforts with other groups would be admirable. Hosting alternative gift fairs, or sharing social media feeds that address these issues — there are many ways of shaping public opinion and targeting income inequality. Finding ways to shape political opinions locally and voting for the most qualified and compassionate candidates are other appropriate actions.

I am sure that at this point it is clear that none of the four strategies are totally separated from the others. Indeed, there are elements of each of the four in many innovative and creative programs that are succeeding in working with people to help them achieve a flourishing life situation. There is much more that could be done and will be done, but let us turn now to some of the good work that can be achieved through government action.

Discussion Questions

1. What individuals and groups influence public opinion locally and on a national level? Do you belong to any of these groups?

2. Consider the values of the U.S. Constitution as those that are upheld by almost all citizens, including the value of citizens' "general welfare." How do you define "general welfare"? Do you think one's definition of "general welfare" tends to be influenced by one's own financial status? What other values may be in conflict with that value?

3. Think about the neighborhood in which you grew up. What sorts of social support (groups, friendships, role models, income, safety, education) were available there? What was lacking?

4. What did the Moving to Opportunity studies reveal about the impact of time spent living in an income-integrated neighborhood rather than a poverty-stricken neighborhood? Drive through the neighborhoods near your church. What do you notice about the social capital of these communities?

5. What prohibits neighbor groups from rehabilitating their entire neighborhood and improving both the social capital and the housing of that neighborhood? How could your church assist in creating a more positive culture in less affluent neighborhoods near you?

6. Can you name some businesses in your area that are helping to improve ALICE's situation, through higher pay or other benefits? How can they change public opinion in regard to employment? How can you help these practices become a cultural norm?

7. Churches have a much larger economic impact than they realize. Can you name three or four? In light of this, what practical steps might the local church take to influence the public opinion of your town or city?

CHAPTER 6

STRATEGY 4:
ADVOCACY AND
GOVERNMENTAL ACTION

We come to the fourth of our strategies: governmental action, which includes laws, policies, and other regulations. Many laws are designed to maintain the safety and security of the American public. But just as the maintenance of roads is taken for granted until roads become treacherous, the lack of support for ALICE and ALEC can go unnoticed until there are protests, strikes, or riots. The earned-income tax credit, Social Security, child-care tax credits, the Affordable Care Act, minimum-wage laws, and free public schools are all governmental policies and programs that benefit ALICE. Some government provisions reflect the strategies of relief (food commodity programs) and self-help (free schools), and most of them are impacted by cultural formation (e.g., subsidization of organic foods and farmers markets). A synergy between the four strategies working together is most effective. Governmental action can reinforce certain cultural values by responding to public opinion. It can indirectly support charity and relief effort, for example, through tax policy; and it can provide incentives for self-help. Every strategy we are considering in chapters 3–6 is tied in with the others; no one of the four could be ignored. What often goes unrecognized is that the achievements of government programs are *our* achievements as voters, taxpayers, and citizen activists.

Governmental programs have also done much to reduce or relieve economic disparities. There are many success stories, for example, surrounding the much-maligned War on Poverty and descendants of that series of initiatives. The most striking success of that "war" perhaps is the reduction of the percentage of American senior citizens in poverty. The rate of the elderly poor has been reduced from 35 percent of older Americans in 1960 to 9 percent in 2012. That 9 percent is five or six points less than the overall national rate of poverty, a remarkable achievement.[1] Supporting that achievement have been the Medicare program for seniors, the Social Security program, the Earned Income Tax Credit, as well as the cultural influence and clout of such groups as the American Association of Retired Persons (AARP). Children have also benefited. Over the past fifty years childhood malnutrition has been significantly reduced, according to the Center on Budget and Policy Priorities.[2] It also appears that nutritionists' efforts are contributing to a reduction in childhood obesity. According to some claims this is due to a significant reduction in the number of high-fructose corn syrup–laden soft drinks children are consuming, thanks to official recommendations against it in certain cities and states.[3] Furthermore, the food stamps program (SNAP) has enabled families and single people living on low incomes to stretch their food budgets. Head Start and other programs highlighted in this book have contributed to leveling the playing field for first-graders.

Other positive programs include Medicaid, a cost-effective way of providing health insurance for low-income Americans and people with disabilities. The Affordable Care Act (Obamacare) has increased the number of Americans who have health insurance and will contribute to a higher level of health, especially for low-income Americans and those workers who do not have insurance through an employer. The ACA is under threat at the moment, and it is difficult to know how seriously it will affect lower-income persons.

There are numerous success stories of government actions that have raised the quality of life for many people; nevertheless, much work remains to be done. Readers can advocate for programs that positively affect ALICE—through boycotts, education and awareness, elections, and contacts with their legislators. In this chapter we will look at government programs in the areas of hunger, wages, health care, climate change, and economic initiatives. The chapter concludes with legislative recommendations for restoring democracy and economic justice.

Lobbying against Hunger

Churches and other humanitarian agencies have been in the forefront of the fight against hunger in the United States and around the world, participating in political lobbying that works to reshape cultural values and press for governmental action.

One such anti-hunger lobbying organization is the Christian organization Bread for the World, which supports domestic efforts to prevent malnourishment among children and mothers in the United States and around the world. A secular organization, the Food and Research Action Center (FRAC), sends out a monthly newsletter that details the positive results of food stamps and also organizations that lobby against cuts in SNAP and other nutritional programs. The Center on Budget and Policy Priorities argues that maintaining social programs that enable the poor and working poor to buy groceries and feed themselves and their children is good policy—not just for asset-limited families but also for the farmers who raise the produce and for the businesses (grocery stores and farmers markets) that benefit from their spending.

Other lobbying organizations include Oxfam; Feeding America; Congressional Hunger Center; No Kid Hungry; Mazon: A Jewish Response to Hunger; Meals on Wheels America; Results: The Power to End Poverty; and Why Hunger? Though the hunger coalition is not the powerhouse that the pork producers, the cattlemen's association, the automotive industry, and some other corporate lobbying groups are, these lobbying organizations work to maintain a stable base that working people can build on.

Legislating a Living Wage

Governmental action is often the result of changes in public opinion and of advocacy groups pressing local, state, and federal legislatures to address particular issues. Chapter 5 mentioned the Fight for $15 as a cultural movement leading to legislative change. The federal minimum wage has been $7.25 since 2006; working full-time at that rate, a person would earn $15,080 a year, still considerably below the poverty level for more than a single person. If that minimum were raised to $15, full-time workers would earn $31,200, which is still in the ALICE category in many areas, but not a desperate income (about $6,000 above the poverty line for a family of four).

The fact that so many states, cities, and the federal government are being pressured to adjust the minimum wage accounts for the progress that some states have made on this front. On July 23, 2015, New York State took the initiative to raise the minimum wage for fast-food workers in New York City to $15 an hour by 2018. This affects 140,000 workers in the city and puts pressure on fast-food companies in other cities to adopt a similar course. The action would be phased in for all fast-food workers in the state by 2021. Already Seattle, San Francisco, and Los Angeles had taken the initiative to raise their minimums to $15, which is considered the minimum for a decent livelihood.[4] The state of

California has acted to do likewise. Furthermore, this will strongly impact other industries and states that are paying low minimums. For this to happen across the country requires legislation, which requires the advocacy of people like you and me.

One of the groups that has been supporting this movement is Wider Opportunities for Women, a nonprofit advocacy organization aimed at boosting income for women and families. They calculated in 2013 that it would take a minimum wage of $14.17 an hour for workers to achieve economic security nationally. Dawn Holmberg is a forty-three-year-old single mother living near Hanson County, South Dakota, one of the places in the United States that has the lowest cost of living—that is, the amount needed to afford economic security. (Economic security is defined as having enough money to afford basic necessities like housing, food, utilities, emergency savings, and child care.) Holmberg earns $10.50 an hour. "We don't do anything; we stay home," she says. "The kids get what they need. Money's tight all the time." At the other end of the scale, in Montgomery County, Maryland, where the cost of living is highest, it takes a wage of at least $23.65 an hour to achieve economic security.[5]

Other income programs are becoming operational. The myRA program, a government-backed retirement plan, was first announced by President Obama in 2014 and has now launched nationally. The myRA is a form of Roth IRA, which allows workers to save their after-tax dollars for retirement. It's intended to overcome some of the obstacles that prevent workers from saving for retirement, especially ALEC and those who lack employer-sponsored retirement benefits. The program charges no fees and is both low-risk and convenient. The money invested would be stored in an account where the principal is backed by the government. Plans are to invest people's money in low-risk instruments with a low interest rate. Of course people must be earning taxable income to use the accounts, which are available to all who are earning less than

$131,000 a year. Perhaps the greatest benefit of such accounts is simply that they will encourage the habit of saving, if only a few dollars a month.[6]

A more far-reaching proposal that is gaining some publicity is a universal basic income (UBI) available to all citizens. A basic income — for example, $10,000 a year given to every citizen over a certain age — would reduce the ill effects of poverty and therefore the cost to society of bad health, crime, and incarceration. In addition, the UBI would signal a respect for enterprises that are certainly work but which go unpaid now. Those who stay at home with children or who give care to the elderly are providing a necessary service; without these services, the society would be much less livable. The UBI is a way of recognizing the value of this labor and is a basic social justice issue. Funding is, of course, an issue: some think that eliminating welfare bureaucracies might offset the cost; others believe that beginning the UBI program at a lower rate and then raising it is feasible. Interesting to me is that similar proposals have been put forward by Thomas Paine (1795!), conservative economists Friedrich Hayek (1960) and Milton Friedman (1962), President Richard Nixon (1969), and Charles Murray of the American Enterprise Institute (2012).

Pushing for Public Health Care

Many groups have pushed for changes in health care on the federal level. Though it may seem as though the Affordable Care Act (also known as Obamacare) has a short history, in fact there have been social movements pressing for health-care reform for at least a century. The International Ladies' Garment Workers' Union established a Union Health Center in New York in 1914, which led them to see the need for more universal provision. In 1915 progressive reformers proposed a system of compulsory health insurance to make up for lost wages and medical costs during sickness. Women trade unionists and suffragists were interested in the plan because it proposed maternity health benefits. In the 1940s President Franklin Roosevelt, the American Federation of Labor (AFL), and the Congress of Industrial Organizations (CIO) pushed for health-care reform. Unions did win health-care benefits from employers during this period. In 1965 Medicare became part of the Social Security Act, and in the 1970s the Committee for National Health Insurance led the drive for universal health care. Efforts for health-care reform were initiated by the Reagan and Clinton administrations. The civil rights movement, the women's movement, and movements on behalf of people with particular diseases, such as AIDS, have worked for change in the health-care system. More recently there have been state-based efforts for reform in places like Maine, Maryland, and Massachusetts.

All these efforts have kept the drive for health-care reform vigorous. In 2010 President Obama proposed the Affordable Care Act and the Health Care and Education Reconciliation Act. It provided a patient's bill of rights and sought to expand health-care coverage to those who were uninsured or could not afford insurance. It sought to reduce the costs of health care. It did away with insurers' prohibitions on pre-existing conditions and instituted a lifetime payment cap on medical bills. Furthermore it extended children's eligibility to be on their parents' policies until their twenty-sixth birthday. In March 2015 the Centers for Disease Control and Prevention reported that the number of uninsured persons was 11.4 million fewer than it had been in 2010. Gallup reported that the percentage of uninsured adults dropped from 18 percent in the third quarter of 2013 to 11.4 percent in the second quarter of 2015.[7] The results state by state vary with the extent to which they have embraced provisions of Obamacare. It is quite clear that the results of the implementation of Obamacare were quite positive in 2016—especially for working-class and low-income people.

Reversing Climate Change
without Job Loss

It is now widely recognized that working-class and lower-income peoples will be the first to feel the results of a warming climate, if they are not already. Rising sea levels, water pollution, environmental racism, and health hazards are well-known effects. What is not well known is that measures taken to reverse climate change can lead to job creation. As more people see the urgency of addressing climate change, there will be new jobs that could employ ALEC at a decent wage.

Many groups have been lobbying Congress to work on climate change. One of those, the Catholic Climate Covenant, has met in a number of states, and its bishops are urging Congress to pass standards that would regulate the emissions of coal-fired power plants. Such power plants are the number one emitter of greenhouse gases in the country.

In August 2015 President Obama built on the experience of the past success of the Environmental Defense Fund in devising a market-based plan, now known as cap-and-trade, to reduce sulfur dioxide emissions. While it set emission targets, it did not tell power companies how to achieve them. And it provided incentives for companies to achieve reduction goals. The Clean Power Plan, formalizing some tough new rules from the Environmental Protection Agency, was aimed at reducing the carbon emitted by power companies. The goal was that by 2030, carbon emissions would be reduced by 32 percent from their 2005 level. The future of President Obama's Clean Power Plan is very tenuous as of April 2017. President Trump ordered the EPA to withdraw the Clean Power Plan and ignore evidence of climate change. Trump also announced his intention to slash the EPA's budget by nearly one third.[8] The administration's perspective seems to be that any regulation will inhibit industry and economic growth, but with creative solutions, new standards that protect global health can also create new jobs.

A report by Global Union Research Network (GURN) suggests that employment sectors need to turn their attention to the questions of mitigation of climate change and transition to new energy sources. It cites a United Nations Environment Programme report, "Green Jobs: Towards Decent Work in a Sustainable, Low-Carbon World," that describes how working to reverse climate change is "generating new jobs in many sectors and economies." The report, which is generally optimistic about the possibility of creating new jobs, argues that the way those environmental jobs are implemented should benefit rather than negatively affect lower-income groups.[9]

The conclusion of the GURN report asserts that the labor market needs to make sure that transitional measures comply with the core principles of sustainable development: "environmental protection, social development and economic growth." Without governmental regulation and labor market efforts, "unemployment and poverty may increase."[10] This transition to new, green jobs might be an opportune time to rethink the level of compensation and the significance of a changing and emerging economy.

Restoring Economic Incentives

There have been numerous suggestions from prestigious commissions of experts that aim to raise middle-class income and pull working-class incomes above the poverty level. One such panel, the Commission on Inclusive Prosperity, produced a report sponsored by the Center for American Progress which recommends that to get "income rising again, workers need more power and education — and companies need better incentives." The goal is to produce better outcomes universally rather than targeting only certain segments of the economy. Besides the to-be-expected recommendations for raising the minimum wage and bolstering labor unions, the report leads off with ideas on how to expand profit sharing. It also endorses several changes in the tax code meant to influence corporate behavior.

For example, it suggests disincentives to high executive compensation, which has a demoralizing effect, and changes to the capital gains taxes at a certain level—two recommendations that would not be disastrous to the wealthy and would be a boon to those who live outside the possibility of capital gains and executive compensation.[11]

Another proposal that has received a great deal of attention is the Atkinson report,[12] which proposes to reduce inequalities in Britain but applies as well to the United States. While it shares many features of the myRA and UBI policies, it does incorporate two features worth highlighting: along with recommending a higher minimum wage, it also commends a guarantee of government employment up to thirty-five hours a week to address unemployment and the proliferation of unstable hourly jobs that make earning a living so erratic.

Related to Atkinson's proposals is that of Gene B. Sperling, who suggests a 401(k) retirement savings plan for all citizens.[13] One way of encouraging savings would be to institute a flat tax credit giving every working American "a 28 percent tax credit for savings, regardless of income." Furthermore, we could institute a 401(k) for everyone through a government-funded universal 401(k) giving "lower- and moderate- income Americans a dollar-for-dollar matching credit for up to $4,000 saved annually per household." Workers could "opt out" if they chose to do so. "President Clinton put forward a similar USA Account proposal in 1999 and President Obama has promoted automatic savings proposals since 2009."[14]

The government is involved in the struggle for economic justice and must focus on restoring economic incentives across the board. There have been suggestions that would "soak the rich." Our intention here, in contrast, has been to point to programs and strategies that benefit all people without targeting the wealthy. Programs that are universally applicable are far more appealing and effective than those that target a specific audience. There have been, to be sure, suggestions for restoring economic fairness such as stopping corporations from using offshore tax havens to avoid U.S. taxes and ending tax breaks for big oil, gas, and coal companies. Another is to tax capital gains and dividends the same as salaries. Senator Bernie Sanders recommended an equity program that applies to all people who contribute to Social Security. His suggestion is to remove the cap that limits the amount of income subject to the Social Security tax to $113,700. This really does make sense as a matter of universal equity. Indeed it is difficult to imagine a counterargument that can be sustained in 2017.

Choosing Democratic Change

One of the values Americans most prize is democracy. We value the fact that everyone in this country has a voice in choosing how we will be governed. But many people are disillusioned with our political system. They feel disenfranchised as the system seems to respond to moneyed interests rather than to the electorate. Of course, the victory of Donald Trump is interpreted as the result of white ALICEs' and ALECs' sense of disenfranchisement and the desire for change. The number of rural and white men and women without a college degree who voted for President Trump suggests a reaction generated by the feeling that the country is being run from corporate boardrooms and by an economic elite.[15]

It is clear that the arrangement of economic laws regulating unions, trusts, banks, wages, and taxes did not descend from God or nature. Laws are passed by legislators; legislators are elected. Collectively, over time, we as a society have chosen to prioritize tax shelters over minimum wages. We have supported an economic system in which the annual bonuses of that tiny percentage of Americans who work just in finance and just in New York City equal *twice* the combined year-round earnings of all Americans earning the federal minimum wage.[16] Congress is anything but representative of the income distribution in the United States. The legislators are politicians whose election and reelection depend on the virtually unlimited contributions of the wealthy allowed by the Supreme

Court's *Citizens United* decision. They themselves enjoy a level of financial security that means that they will never begin to experience the situation of the ALICEs and ALECs. Though it is legal, it is clear that the wealthy have a hugely disproportionate voice in who gets elected and what policies they support. That has become increasingly evident, and the repeal of *Citizens United* is a key link in reempowering the electorate, especially the bottom 80 percent.

Parker Palmer, social commentator and theologian, underscores the interrelation of the political and the economic in America; he believes that one of the costs of economic inequality is the erosion of democratic values. He writes, "If American democracy fails, the ultimate cause will not be a foreign invasion or the power of big money or the greed and dishonesty of some elected officials. . . . It will happen because we—you and I—became so fearful of each other, of our differences and of the future, that we unraveled the civic community on which democracy depends, losing our power to resist all that threatens it and call it back to its highest form."[17]

The increasing centralization of power to influence government and the decline of civic empowerment go hand in hand. Palmer points toward demoralization among the working class (and lower-income and middle class), which springs from the sense of not having a voice in the way we are governed. At the heart of civic vigor is the sense of empowerment that the citizens of a community have. An ability to participate in decision making contributes to happiness and a sense of purpose.[18] This is what we referred to earlier as "social capital"—participation in the group aspects of life in community, the sense of having a place or belonging. Essential to this sense of having a place is trust, being engaged in a way that makes a difference in an organization or social group, a sense of being able to contribute. Having a job, and especially a decent job, is tied to one's sense of making a contribution.

Nobel laureate Joseph Stiglitz notes another political impact of the centralization of power when he asserts that "inequality is a matter not so much of *capitalism* in the 20th century as of *democracy* in the 20th century."[19] The centralization of power tends to insulate legislators from being affected by the interests of the working class (and the lower-income and middle class) and produces a lack of trust. In short, the electorate sense that their opinion no longer matters. The electorate do not feel that the government or either political party cares about them, and they seem to have a point. When we do not trust the government, we tend to become disillusioned with "democracy" and feel disempowered.

Restoring Economic Justice

The spiraling effect of these two forces—loss of participation and lack of trust—is especially evident among African Americans and Latinos. Police officers killed Michael Brown in Ferguson, Missouri, and other black men in Cleveland, North Charleston, New York City, Baltimore, and elsewhere in 2015. This is no way to build civic engagement or trust among African Americans. Paul Krugman worries that the "centrality of race and racism" in news about police shootings might lead people to assume that desperate poverty and estrangement from society are uniquely African American experiences, when actually "much though by no means all of the horror one sees in Baltimore and many other places is really about class, about the devastating effects of extreme and rising inequality."[20] Krugman cites William Julius Wilson, a black sociologist who argues that "widely-decried social changes among blacks . . . were . . . caused by the disappearance of well-paying jobs in inner cities." His claim carries the implication that if other groups lost job opportunities, "their behavior would change in similar ways."[21] And that has proved to be true. White rates of infant mortality, lack of educational achievement, crime, stagnant wages, divorce, drug use, and single parenthood are also rising and are found disproportionately in poor and working-class neighborhoods. Nationwide, mortality rates and life expectancy increasingly reflect the widening gap between rich and poor.

Furthermore, it is becoming clear that the entire economy is being negatively affected by the gulf between socioeconomic classes. If we take infant mortality as a key index, what drives the point home is that the infant mortality rate in the United States is twice as high as in Germany. "American babies born to white, college-educated, married women survive as often as those born to advantaged women in Europe. It's the babies born to nonwhite, nonmarried, nonprosperous women who die so young." The United States ranks at or near the bottom of high-income countries in life expectancy and mortality. We have the highest teenage birthrate—seven times that of France. We also have the largest percentage of children living with one parent, and one child in five lives in poverty. In addition, the country has a very high rate of incarceration, and by some measures we have a general sense of a lack of well-being and prosperity. All these social facts can be put at the feet of "excess inequality." We are talking about ALEC here. Furthermore, these rates are moving in the wrong direction; in comparison with U.S. rates in 1980, some have actually declined. Certainly related is the fact that over forty or so years, the U.S. "labor market lost much of its power to deliver income gains to working families."[22]

It is becoming overwhelmingly obvious that the wealth of everyone is based on our connections and dependence on one another. Indexes indicate that rising economic insecurity is hurting our economy. For one thing, the inability among many to consume because of economic constraints means that our economy cannot grow at the rate that is expected. The reduction of social mobility is another problem. The government and taxpayers (we!) are picking up the tab for those companies and other organizations that do not pay a living wage and whose employees are therefore eligible for SNAP benefits, low-earner tax credits, subsidized lunch programs for their children, and other welfare programs. Without a living wage, ALICE, ALEC, and the poor will depend on governmental or private aid, which ultimately comes out of the pockets of the same people unwilling to pay the slightly higher prices

Resources for Supporting Governmental Action

Government has the power to establish or change policies and finance the programs it sponsors or endorses, but we the people have the power to influence our lawmakers by advocating for policies and programs that promote income equality.

Contact your representatives at all levels of government, from your city council to the statehouse to your senators and congresspersons in Washington, DC. Find their contact information online. https://www.usa.gov/elected-officials/

Calling representatives' offices is the most effective way to be heard, but e-mails can make a difference too. The **United Way** offers an easy online form to automatically contact your representatives regarding certain issues. https://www.unitedway.org/get-involved/take-action

Support the lobbying actions of the **Fight for $15 movement** and other state and local actions to raise the minimum wage. http://www.fightfor15.org

Support **Bread for the World**, which advocates for legislation that will alleviate hunger. They have many local chapters throughout the United States. http://www.bread.org

that would help employers justify paying higher wages. The greater the ranks of those who are able to achieve a decent standard of living, the more families and children will benefit and potentially break the cycle of poverty for generation after generation that produces hopelessness, frustration, and disillusionment with the American dream.

Governmental policy and programs are an indispensable strategy for addressing income inequality. Our calling to support those who are committed to ending poverty, enabling ALEC to live decently, and ensuring a good quality of life for everyone requires our political participation as we take action to demand justice for all.

Discussion Questions

1. It is clear that local, state, and federal levels of government shape our lives. What are the assets and liabilities of that influence? Where are you most conscious of that influence? Are there areas where the government is too much involved? Areas where it is neglecting its responsibility?

2. Are economic incentives always necessary for businesses to choose policies that benefit workers or the environment? How can greater economic security for the working class and poor improve the economy for everyone?

3. Can you imagine the consequences of paying every worker a minimum wage of $15 an hour? How would that affect workers' family life and civic engagement, for example? Might the impact of that minimum wage extend to the next generation—workers' children?

4. What if the United States established a universal basic income of $10,000 a year, or adopted the Atkinson plan guaranteeing government employment up to thirty-five hours a week for those who wanted it? What would be the liabilities of such programs? What would be the benefits?

5. What would it take to make the reversal of climate change a boon to ALICE and ALEC? Could this happen without governmental action?

6. If there were a universal basic income or increased minimum wage in the United States, what would be their impact on the public's feeling of engagement with the political process? Would voting percentages improve and involvement in city and county politics expand to include more citizen participation?

7. Why do you think the measures of social well-being are declining in the United States? How could those declines be reversed?

8. How might you get more involved in reshaping governmental priorities? Do you vote? Contact your legislators by phone or e-mail? Attend city council meetings? Would you ever consider running for office?

9. How could you help ALICE and ALEC be more involved in the political process? What would enhance feelings of engagement and empowerment?

CHAPTER 7

GETTING STARTED

In this study, we have focused on programs and policies that are in agreement with Christian values and that work to alleviate the conditions that make for poverty, that stabilize the lives of the working poor (ALICE and ALEC), and that address the problem of a shrinking middle class. Rather than seeking to analyze the reasons for the widening gap between rich and poor, we prefer to lift up strategies for repairing the gap and to highlight organizations and programs that are hard at work doing so. The previous four chapters have dealt extensively with programs, projects, initiatives, and other activities that attempt to alleviate income inequality. This final chapter will help you integrate strategies for promoting others' material flourishing into your everyday faith and the mission of your congregation or group.

While the activities we commend have concentrated on raising ALEC's income level, the ultimate goal is to promote human flourishing, a vitality of spirit that includes an adequate material base and the recognition of one's dignity and value. Do not underestimate the value of simply listening and empathizing with those in need. Responding to another's concerns in the appropriate way depends on this empathetic listening. Working together for the good of all brings us joy and brings dignity and a sense of worthiness to the working poor. It is difficult to imagine a more gratifying or long-lasting source of flourishing.

We have covered a lot of ground in these six chapters and discussed many economic and political factors that may, on the surface, feel unrelated to Christian faith. But we know that promoting the good life for everyone—especially for our neighbors who struggle economically—is an essential Christian practice, as much a part of spiritual life as prayer and worship. Indeed, these practices are intertwined. The two great commandments—love God and love neighbor—should not be seen as obligations but as graciously given guides to the lifestyles that will lead naturally to our human fulfillment and joy.

While we are striving to practice the mercy and justice expected of us as Christians, it is important that our congregations and other groups approach ministry to the poor and working poor with all four strategies in mind. We are called to practice charity, meeting immediate needs so that people can go on to thrive. We are called to assist and empower others in ways that will eventuate in their own self-determination and success. We are called to advocate for cultural values that will foster generosity and promote equality for all, especially for those with fewer resources. Finally, we need to work to encourage the enactment of legislation that will solidify and expand the possibilities for the empowerment of ALICE. Lest this sound too intimidating, you will recall that many strategies are intertwined, combining elements of self-help as a follow-up to relief efforts, for example, or cultural formation as a tactic for influencing political policy. No church can do everything. That is fine. There are ways of addressing unstable life situations for ALEC that fit your context and that are within your capacities.

The prompts and exercises that make up the remainder of this chapter will help you assess your current ministries, recognize budding passions, and identify untapped resources in light of the four strategies. The recommendations in chapters 3–6 for identifying local and national organizations that employ the different strategies should have given you a head start in developing your plan for ongoing ministry. Now is the time for discernment and bold vision, strategizing ways that your congregation can proceed from this study to promote the good life for all people in your community and the nation as a whole. Godspeed in your discernment process.

Assessing Your Current Ministries

Make a list of your congregation's current programs that benefit the poor and working poor. After each item on the list, mark which strategy or strategies this ministry utilizes (R = relief, S = self-help, C = cultural formation, G = governmental action and advocacy).

Name of program	R	S	C	G

1. Do you notice any trends in which strategies your church's ministries seem to use? Is there a conscious reason for this trend, or has it happened naturally? What strengths of your congregation do you see reflected in this list?

2. Do you see any opportunities for a shift or expansion of strategies in any of the ministries listed? (For example, if you have an active ministry of relief for the homeless, could you also lobby your elected officials concerning policies affecting the homeless in your community?)

3. What might be keeping you from attempting the strategies that are represented less or not at all on your list? Do these reflect a certain challenge for your congregation?

4. Are there any programs you are currently doing that need strengthening or expansion? Are there any that need to be reassessed?

Areas of Need

Consider the needs listed on this page. Circle those already being addressed by ministries in your church. Put a box around those that you do not currently address but see a need for in your immediate community. Put a star by those you feel particularly passionate about or feel you have particular skills to offer (whether they are circled, boxed, or neither).

Adult literacy

Affordable child care

Clothing

Disaster relief

Elder care

Employment

English as an additional language

Financial literacy

Health and safety

Homelessness

Home repairs

Hunger

Kindergarten readiness

Living wage

Maternal/infant care

Mentoring

Refugee resettlement

Substance abuse

Tutoring

Working conditions

1. Analyze your circled items for a moment. Do you notice any trends in the types of needs (immediate, education-focused, etc.) or types of people (children, immigrants, etc.) you currently serve? Are these trends an asset, or do they reveal a challenge?

2. Were there any boxes, indicating gaps between your ministries and the needs of your community? Were any of those boxes starred?

3. What needs do you feel passionate about or particularly equipped for meeting? Are there several people in the group who feel a similar calling to a certain type of ministry?

4. Can you think of any individuals in your congregation who are not part of this study group who have shown a passion or skill that would be useful in meeting an underserved need on this list?

5. One spiritual practice, perhaps somewhat overlooked, is simply listening and developing empathy with human need. How might empathetic listening help us respond appropriately to others' needs?

Partnering and Planning

Looking over your insights from the previous two exercises, name three to five issues that need further consideration. These might include current ministries that need expanding or reassessing, untried strategies that might need pursuing, or unmet needs in your community.

1.

2.

3.

4.

5.

About each, ask the following questions:

1. Are there organizations or resources identified in chapters 3–6 that we might investigate for help or potential partnership?

2. Are there individuals we know in our congregation or the community who could add valuable insight as we plan our next steps?

3. Who will be the point person for this issue? What is our next step in considering this change or addition to our ministries to the poor and working poor?

These questions and those throughout this resource are by no means exhaustive; they are intended to encourage your own planning and exploration. While it is doubtful that one church or organization could do everything, it is always possible for one group to do something—and many churches and other organizations operating together can do much more than any single one could. May God bless your thinking and working!

NOTES

Introduction

1. David P. King, "Shaping a Theology of Money," *Faith and Leadership*, March 24, 2015, https://www.faithandleadership.com/david-p-king-shaping-theology-money.

Chapter 1   Interdependence and the Working Poor

1. Paul Buchheit, "Half of America Is In or Damn Near Close to Living in Poverty," AlterNet, December 14, 2015, http://www.alternet.org/economy/half-america-or-damn-near-close-living-poverty.

2. Kathleen Gray, *Detroit Free Press*, "Jeb Bush in Detroit: Americans Have Right to Rise Out of Poverty," *Bradenton Herald*, February 5, 2015.

3. Mark R. Rank and Thomas A. Hirschl, "Calculate Your Economic Risk," *New York Times*, March 20, 2016, National edition, SR9.

4. Mark Wiedmer, "Community Kitchen Making Us All Thankful," *Chattanooga Times Free Press*, November 26, 2015.

5. Joseph E. Stiglitz, *The Price of Inequality* (New York: W. W. Norton, 2012).

6. "Ending Child Poverty Now," Children's Defense Fund report, January 28, 2015, quoted by Charles M. Blow, "Reducing Our Obscene Level of Child Poverty," *New York Times*, January 28, 2015, https://www.nytimes.com/2015/01/28/opinion/charles-blow-reducing-our-obscene-level-of-child-poverty.html.

7. Children's Defense Fund, "Ending Child Poverty Now." See more at http://www.childrensdefense.org/library/PovertyReport/EndingChildPovertyNow.html.

8. Pope Francis, *Laudato Si'* ("On Care for Our Common Home"), papal encyclical promulgated May 25, 2015, paragraph 16.

9. Excerpted in "How to Spread the World's Wealth beyond Corrupt Elites," Alternet, November 30, 2015, http://www.alternet.org/books/how-spread-worlds-wealth-beyond-corrupt-elites.

Chapter 2   Toward a Spirituality of Flourishing

1. Henri J. M. Nouwen, *Lifesigns: Intimacy, Fecundity, and Ecstasy in Christian Perspective* (New York: Doubleday, 1989), 96–97.

2. Sue McGregor, "Consumerism as a Source of Structural Violence," 2003, http://www.kon.org/hswp/archive/consumerism.pdf. Quoted in Dawn Nothwehr, *Ecological Footprints: An Essential Franciscan Guide for Faith and Sustainable Living* (Collegeville, MN: Liturgical Press, 2012), 172.

3. On the interdependence of self and other, see Shannon Jung, "Autonomy as Justice: Spatiality and the Revelation of Otherness," *Journal of Religious Ethics* 14, no. 1 (Spring 1986): 157–83.

4. Richard Dymond, "Sarasota Family Turns Stolen Bicycles into Act of Kindness," *Bradenton Herald*, January 31, 2015, http://www.bradenton.com/news/local/article34789137.html.

5. Christine Pohl, *Making Room: Recovering Hospitality as a Christian Tradition* (Grand Rapids: Eerdmans, 1999), 74.

6. Yadira Lopez, "Helping Women Reclaim Their Lives," *Bradenton Herald*, March 18, 2016.

7. Nothwehr, *Ecological Footprints*, 170–83.

8. Christian Smith and Hilary Davidson, *The Paradox of Generosity: Giving We Receive, Grasping We Lose* (New York: Oxford University Press, 2014), 4, 44–45.

9. Ibid., 97.

10. E. J. Dionne, "The Discipline of Gratitude," *Chattanooga Times Free Press*, November 23, 2015.

11. Martin Copenhaver, "Learning to Give Thanks," *Christian Century*, October 30, 2015, 35.

12. Ibid.

13. Nouwen, *Lifesigns*, 35.

Chapter 3   Strategy 1: Relief

1. For dramatic insights into payday loans and other aspects of living on the edge, see Linda Tirado, *Hand to Mouth: Living in Bootstrap America*

(New York: G. P. Putnam's Sons, 2014); Kathryn J. Edin and H. Luke Shaefer, *$2.00 a Day: Living On Almost Nothing in America* (Boston: Houghton Mifflin Harcourt, 2015); and David K. Shipler, *The Working Poor: Invisible in America* (New York: Vintage Books, Random House, 2005).

2. Caitlin Ashworth, "Summit Focuses on Hunger in Region," *Sarasota-Manatee Herald Tribune*, September 30, 2015, http://www.heraldtribune.com /article/20150930/article/150939961.

3. Steve Corbett and Brian Fikkert, *When Helping Hurts: How to Alleviate Poverty without Hurting the Poor and Yourself* (Chicago: Moody Publishers, 2012), 61.

4. Karl M. Gaspar, *Desperately Seeking God's Saving Action: Yolanda Survivors' Hope beyond Heartbreaking Lamentations* (Philippines: Institute of Spirituality in Asia, 2014).

5. Ibid., 51.

6. Ibid., 92.

Chapter 4   Strategy 2: Self-Help

1. Ramesh Ponnuru, "Let's Not Mention Inequality," *New York Times*, February 9, 2015, https://www.nytimes.com/2015/02/09/opinion/lets-not -mention-inequality.html

2. Emily Ekins, "Poll: 74 Percent Say Congress Should Prioritize Economic Growth Over Reducing Income Inequality," *Reason.com*, October 2, 2014, http://reason.com/poll/2014/10/02/poll-74-percent-say-congress -should-prio.

3. Neil Irwin, "Why Americans Don't Want to Soak the Rich," *New York Times*, April 17, 2015, https://www.nytimes.com/2015/04/19/upshot /why-americans-dont-want-to-soak-the-rich.html

4. E. J. Dionne Jr., "Obama, Overtime, and the Value of Hard Work," *Washington Post*, July 1, 2015, https://www.washingtonpost.com/opinions /how-much-do-we-value-work/2015/07/01/081b614c-2023-11e5-aeb9 -a411a84c9d55_story.html?utm_term=.0c87249f1bfd.

5. Vin Mannix, "For 20 Years, Bradenton Nonprofit Has Been Shining the 'Light,'" *Bradenton Herald*, March 5, 2014, http://www.bradenton .com/news/local/news-columns-blogs/article34708719.html

6. Nicholas Kristof, "Oklahoma! Where the Kids Learn Early," *New York Times*, Sunday Review, November 10, 2013, http://www.nytimes.com /2013/11/10/opinion/sunday/kristof-oklahoma-where-the-kids-learn-early .html.

7. Monika Hellwig, *The Eucharist and the Hunger of the World*, 2nd ed. (Franklin, WI: Sheed & Ward, 1992), 13.

8. Greg Kaufmann, interview by Bill Moyers, "America's Poor Are Demonized to Justify Huge Cuts in Government Programs," June 28, 2013, http://www.alternet.org/news-amp-politics/greg-kaufmann-american -poverty. The interview originally appeared on BillMoyers.com.

9. "Food Insecurity and Hunger in the U.S.: New Research," Food Research and Action Center and Children's Healthwatch, April 29, 2015.

10. Kaufmann interview.

11. Soo Oh, "Low-Income Americans Can No Longer Afford Rent, Food, and Transportation," *Vox*, March 30, 2016, http://www.vox.com/2016 /3/30/11330832/low-income-households-cant-afford-basic-needs. Mark R. Rank and Thomas A. Hirschl report that "a clear majority of Americans will experience poverty. For example, in earlier research we estimated that between the ages of 20 and 75, nearly 60 percent of Americans will spend at least one year below the official poverty line, and three-quarters will experience a year below 150 percent of the poverty line." Rank and Hirschl, "Calculate Your Economic Risk," *New York Times*, Sunday Review, March 20, 2016, https://www.nytimes.com/2016/03/20/opinion/sunday/calculate -your-economic-risk.html.

12. "Supplemental Nutrition Assistance Program (SNAP)," U.S. Department of Agriculture Food and Nutrition Service, http://www.fns .usda.gov/snap/eligibility, accessed February 25, 2017.

13. Kaufmann interview.

14. Rachel Crosby, "New Homeless Center Lets Residents Get Back On Their Feet," *Tampa Bay Times*, February 6, 2015.

15. Amanda Ripley, "How to Graduate from Starbucks," *Atlantic*, May 2015, 60–72.

16. Ibid., 66.

17. Ibid., 68, 72.

18. David Bornstein, "Overcoming Poverty's Damage to Learning," *New York Times*, Opinion Pages, April 17, 2015, https://opinionator.blogs .nytimes.com/2015/04/17/overcoming-povertys-damage-to-learning/?emc.

19. Ibid.

20. Ibid.

21. Emma Brown, "This Superintendent Has Figured Out How to Make School Work for Poor Kids," *Washington Post*, December 20, 2015, https://www.washingtonpost.com/local/education/this-superintendent

-has-figured-out-how-to-make-school-work-for-poor-kids/2015/12
/20/cadac2ca-a4e6-11e5-ad3f-991ce3374e23_story.html?utm_term=
.dc4644909074.

22. Ron Haskins, "Social Programs That Work," *New York Times*, January 1, 2105.

23. David L. Kirp, "What Do the Poor Need? Try Asking Them," *New York Times*, August 8, 2015, https://www.nytimes.com/2015/08/09/opinion
/sunday/david-l-kirp-what-do-the-poor-need-try-asking-them.html.

24. Catherine A. Heaney and Barbara A. Israel, "Social Networks and Social Support," in *Health Behavior and Health Education: Theory, Research, and Practice*, ed. Karen Glanz, Barbara K. Rimer, and K. Viswaneth (San Francisco: John Wiley & Sons, 2008), 205–6.

25. See David Bornstein, "Out of Poverty, Family-Style," *New York Times*, Opinionator, July 14, 2011, http://opinionator.blogs.nytimes.com
/2011/07/14/out-of-poverty-family-style/?pagemode.

26. Laura Pappano, "First-Generation Students Unite," *New York Times*, Education Life, April 8, 2015, https://www.nytimes.com/2015/04/12
/education/edlife/first-generation-students-unite.html?emc=edi.

Chapter 5 Strategy 3: Cultural Formation

1. Nelson D. Schwartz, "Starbucks and Other Corporations to Announce Plan to Curb Unemployment of Young People," *New York Times*, July 13, 2015, https://www.nytimes.com/2015/07/13/business/starbucks-and
-other-corporations-to-announce-plan-to-curb-unemployment-of-young
-people.html.

2. Steven Greenhouse, "How the $15 Minimum Wage Went from Laughable to Viable," *New York Times*, Sunday Review, April 1, 2016, https://
www.nytimes.com/2016/04/03/sunday-review/how-the-15-minimum-wage
-went-from-laughable-to-viable.html.

3. Amy Bennett Williams, "For Florida Tomato Workers, Extra Penny Really Adds Up," *Bradenton Herald*, February 22, 2014.

4. Cornelia Butler Flora and Jan L. Flora, *Rural Communities: Legacy and Change* (Boulder CO: Westview Press, 2016).

5. Robert D. Putnam, *Our Kids: The American Dream in Crisis* (New York: Simon & Schuster, 2015).

6. Catherine A. Heaney and Barbara A. Israel, "Social Networks and Social Support," in *Health Behavior and Health Education: Theory, Research, and*

Practice, ed. Karen Glanz, Barbara K. Rimer, and K. Viswaneth (San Francisco: John Wiley & Sons, 2008), 189–207.

7. Ibid., 198.

8. Matthew Desmond, *Evicted: Poverty and Profit in the American City* (New York: Crown Publishers, 2016).

9. Tina Rosenberg, *Join the Club: How Peer Pressure Can Transform the World* (New York: W. W. Norton, 2012).

10. Charles Murray, *Coming Apart: The State of White America, 1960–2010* (New York: Crown Forum, Random House, 2012).

11. See Patti Neighmond, "Improving Housing Can Pay Dividends in Better Health," NPR, March 3, 2015, http://www.npr.org/sections/health -shots/2015/03/03/389320510/improving-housing-can-pay-dividends-in -better-health?utm_campaign=storyshare&utm_source=twitter.com&utm _medium=social. The report about Bridge Housing appears there and also in http://www.bridgehousing.com.

12. See Josh Salman, "Affordable Housing Is a Challenge Here," *Sarasota-Manatee Herald Tribune*, April 13, 2015.

13. "The Best and Worst Places to Grow Up: How Your Area Compares," *New York Times*, May 4, 2015, https://www.nytimes.com/interactive /2015/05/03/upshot/the-best-and-worst-places-to-grow-up-how-your-area -compares.html.

14. Raj Chetty, Nathaniel Hendren, and Lawrence F. Katz, "The Effects of Exposure to Better Neighborhoods on Children: New Evidence from the Moving to Opportunity Experiment," August 2015, available at http://www .equality-of-opportunity.org/documents/; published in *American Economic Review* 106:4 (April 2016): 855–902. Their work was reported by Justin Wolfers, "Why the New Research on Mobility Matters: An Economist's View," The Upshot, *New York Times*, May 4, 2015, https://www.nytimes.com/2015/05/05 /upshot/why-the-new-research-on-mobility-matters-an-economists-view.html.

15. Personal e-mail, January 28, 2015. See also Elaine A. Heath and Larry Duggins, *Missional, Monastic, Mainline: A Guide to Starting Missional Microcommunities in Historically Mainline Traditions* (Eugene, OR: Cascade, 2014).

16. 100,000 Opportunities Initiative, https://www.100kopportunities .org/.

17. David Morris, "Success Stories from San Francisco Prove That Retailers Profit More When They Treat Their Workers Fairly," Alternet, December 15, 2014, http://www.alternet.org/labor/success-stories-san -francisco-prove-retailers-profit-more-when-they-treat-their-workers-fairly.

18. Ibid.

19. Paul Krugman, "Liberals and Wages," *New York Times*, July 17, 2015, https://www.nytimes.com/2015/07/17/opinion/paul-krugman-liberals -and-wages.html.

20. Paul Keegan, "Does More Pay Mean More Growth?," *Inc.*, November 2015, 70.

21. Ibid., 71, 76.

22. Suzanne Anarde, "Investing in Strong Rural Communities," *American Banking Association Journal*, August 25, 2015, http://bankingjournal.aba .com/2015/08/investing-in-strong-rural-communities/.

23. Eduardo Porter, "Corporate Efforts to Address Social Problems Have Limits," September 8, 2015, https://www.nytimes.com/2015/09/09 /business/economy/corporate-efforts-to-address-social-problems-have -limits.html?_r=0.

24. Ibid.

25. Mary Mazzoni, "10 U.S. Companies That Pay Above Minimum Wage," *Triple Pundit*, Feb. 28, 2014, http://www.triplepundit.com/2014/02 /3p-weekend-10-companies-pay-living-wage/; Jenny Che, "13 Companies That Aren't Waiting for Congress to Raise the Minimum Wage," *Huffington Post*, April 2, 2015, http://www.huffingtonpost.com/2015/04/02/companies -minimum-wage_n_6991672.html.

Chapter 6   Strategy 4:
Advocacy and Governmental Action

1. "Safety Net Successes," *Christian Century*, February 5, 2014, 7.

2. Ibid.

3. James B. Stewart, "For Coke, the Challenge Is Staying Relevant," *New York Times*, February 28, 2014.

4. "A Big Victory for Fast-Food Workers in New York," *New York Times*, July 23, 2015, https://www.nytimes.com/2015/07/24/opinion/a-big -victory-for-fast-food-workers-in-new-york.html.

5. Jillian Berman, "$10.20 Per Hour Needed to Survive Even in America's Cheapest County," *Huffington Post*, updated July 18, 2013, http:// www.huffingtonpost.com/2013/07/17/worker-wage_n_3610530.html.

6. Jonnelle Marte, "Saving for Retirement Is About to Get a Little Easier for Some Workers," *Washington Post*, November 4, 2015.

7. The description of the act and its results is drawn from U.S. Department of Health and Human Services, https://www.hhs.gov/healthcare /about-the-law/index.html, accessed on August 7, 2015; from an Associated

Press report on March 24, 2015; and from Stephanie Marken, "U.S. Uninsured Rate at 11.4% in Second Quarter," Gallup-Healthways Well-Being Index, July 10, 2015, http://www.gallup.com/poll/184064/uninsured -rate-second-quarter.aspx?g_source=&g_medium=&g_campaign=tiles.

8. Scott K. Johnson, "Trump Kills Clean Power Plan, Orders Agencies to Ignore Climate Change," Ars Technica, March 28, 2017, https:// arstechnica.com/science/2017/03/trumps-executive-order-on-climate-change -finally-drops/.

9. This legislation has been judicially blocked. On the employment implications of this act, see Lene Olsen, "The Employment Effects of Climate Change and Climate Change Responses: A Role for International Labour Standards?" (discussion paper, Global Union Research Network, International Labor Office, Geneva, 2009), http://empleosverdes.mex.ilo.org/wp-content /uploads/2013/10/The-Employment-Effects-of-Climate-Change-and -Climate-Change-Responses-A-Role-for-International-Labour-Standards. pdf, 7–8, 24.

10. Ibid., 24.

11. Jim Tankersley, "Helping the Middle Class," *Tampa Bay Times*, January 21, 2015.

12. Anthony B. Atkinson, *Inequality: What Can Be Done?* (Cambridge, MA: Harvard University Press, 2015).

13. Gene B. Sperling, "A 401(k) for All," *New York Times*, July 22, 2014, https://www.nytimes.com/2014/07/23/opinion/a-401-k-for-all.html.

14. Ibid.

15. Edward McClelland, "The Rust Belt Was Turning Red Already. Donald Trump Just Pushed It Along," *Tampa Bay Times*, November 13, 2016. Seventy-two percent of white men without a college degree and 62 percent of people living in a small town or rural area voted for Trump.

16. Tim Worstall, "Fun Number; Wall Street Bonus Pot Is Twice Total Minimum Wage Earnings in the US," *Forbes*, May 3, 2015, http://www .forbes.com/sites/timworstall/2015/05/03/fun-number-wall-street-bonus -pot-is-twice-total-minimum-wage-earnings-in-the-us/#6096579864df.

17. Parker J. Palmer, *Healing the Heart of Democracy: The Courage to Create a Politics Worthy of the Human Spirit* (San Francisco: Jossey-Bass, 2011), 9.

18. See documentation on this in L. Shannon Jung, *Hunger and Happiness: Feeding the Hungry, Nourishing Our Souls* (Minneapolis: Augsburg Books, 2009), 97–100.

19. Quoted by Nicholas Kristof, "Inequality Is a Choice," *New York Times*, Sunday Review, May 3, 2015.

20. Paul Krugman, "Race, Class, and Neglect," *New York Times*, May 4, 2015, https://www.nytimes.com/2015/05/04/opinion/paul-krugman-race -class-and-neglect.html.

21. Ibid.

22. Eduardo Porter, "Income Inequality Is Costing the U.S. on Social Issues," *New York Times*, April 28, 2015, https://www.nytimes.com/2015 /04/29/business/economy/income-inequality-is-costing-the-us-on-social -issues.html.

CPSIA information can be obtained
at www.ICGtesting.com
Printed in the USA
FSOW01n1751190917
38831FS